MW00873252

APR 16 2015

ACLS - Cancel

Art & the Impossible

Godmothers, Grandmothers and a Greater Vision -   A history of Peter Miller, women artists, famous friends, creative spirits, and dreams.

Andrea Miller Theisson

Copyright 2015
Andrea Miller Theisson

CONTENTS

Art and the Impossible

Godmothers, Grandmothers, and a Greater Vision - A history of Peter Miller, women artists, famous friends, creative spirits, and dreams.

Introduction

Like all good stories, this is about what is important, what can make a difference. Life choices have many influences and geography is only one. Connections can transcend distances and life-spans. Women have traditionally mentored and nurtured kindred souls, whether they are blood-relations or spirit-mates. There were years of interviews and correspondence with many special people who knew Peter Miller and her circle. I wish I had started twenty years ago, when more of them remained alive. But, live on they did! The stories and the light that shone for the tellers is a testimony to the power of a creative soul like Peter Miller.

Peter Miller was a complex individual, who cherished her privacy, yet, as most artists, loved to share her work and ideas. She was always authentically herself,

> "There is a fullness and a joy that defines Peter Miller…" Frank H. Goodyear Jr.

and a complicated Self that was. Her work was shown from the East Coast to the West, and back again, in major galleries and museums. Called "metaphysical" in the era of "Magical Realism," her life and work were a blend of mystery and romance, as well as classical empiricism and practicality. She and her friends thought outside the box, long before the expression was heard. This is a book that kept expanding its mission. The years spent thinking about it, meditating on the memories of characters involved, and then actually tracking down, contacting, and interviewing so many other people who knew Peter Miller and her friends were fascinating. Ultimately, it became a book about the Creative Spirit, and about what really matters in life.

> "The creative instinct is…an enormous extra vitality, a super-energy, born inexplicably in an individual…an energy which no single life can consume."
>
> Pearl S. Buck, December 12, 1938 (youngest woman to receive the Nobel Prize in Literature, Art, Writing and Nature of Creativity)

Everyone interviewed, from internationally known art historians to artists and neighbors to her driver and farm worker, lightened-up immediately and smiled about Peter Miller, celebrating her life and personality with stories and more connections to pursue. She primarily wished to stimulate people to think, to express themselves,

> "Painting answers something I need to have asked. "
> Peter Miller

and to collect their experiences, artworks, and thoughts into her own life. She did not see the point in owning anything that was not authentic, original, or simply beautiful. And so I could feel the quality of her life, and how she enjoyed embracing the positive as she rode "lickety split" through her journey on earth. It was too short, indeed, for all of her ideas!

2

Sometimes we all just want something more out of life. Sometimes we must create our own myths. Peter Miller and Jennifer Chapin, two highly creative friends, did this in an authentic and conscious manner. They became modern women in a time of incredible intellectual and social change, and they influenced many others. Creativity can become an all-consuming force to reckon with. Growing up in a small town does not prevent this urge for either the most privileged or the most challenged. We must stretch beyond so many kinds of limits to develop into autonomous souls. Having a foot in two worlds can make us see both of them more clearly.

Is it impossible to combine an art world of famous contacts with intensely private people? Is it impossible to live quietly and productively as an artist and still become known to the world? Is it impossible to be a true artist without an enormous ego? Is it impossible to be a person of privilege AND a woman AND a respected artist? Did revelations of intellect and spirituality ever really become fully acknowledged, or comfortable for women artists? How did the larger social movement of Industrialization and the inevitable backlash dominate artists of the early-mid 20th Century? Peter Miller ran headlong into all of these conflicts and questions.

As an aristocratic non-conformist, Peter lived in the moment, while finding deep connections to a past that she did not expect. She was a very private person. Her journals were to be destroyed when she died, as were her friend Jennifer's. And, as Beth Gates Warren* wrote about Margrethe Mather, another woman artist of the era, "Her mythomania and lifelong penchant for secretiveness make her history a confounding one to reconstruct."

 Indeed, it took over 4 years to piece together even a partial biography, despite my family knowing her well. I will be open to revisions, always! This complex, spiraling written effort is a positive and accurate description of many people I personally knew, with many references to a

Oxford dictionary definition of bohemian:
 "A socially unconventional person, especially one who is involved in the arts."

fascinating body of works already published, and the paintings which they produced. We still have a journal that Peter and Jennifer passed back and forth. They loved quotes! Many included are the ones they collected, some are my own. I discovered what it was like to get mixed messages, keep creating, and to receive much inspiration from so many gifted women from a small town in Pennsylvania. Their links to the New York art world, collectors, Native American peoples and philosophy, nature and conservation, big names and nobodies-who-still-matter, historic movements, and the very roots of women's creativity have affected generations already. It became what it is – a collage of tales. May these stories inspire even more. At least, may this book be a guide to exploring further. It's a wide, wonderful world.

"All human beings are practicing historians – we live our lives, we tell our stories. It is as natural as breathing. But if no one cares about those stories, they do not survive. People not only make history by living their lives, but by creating records and by turning other people's lives into books..."
Gerda Lerner, historian

3

"You use a glass mirror to see your face; you use works of art to see your soul."

George Bernard Shaw

"If you want your life to be a magnificent story, then begin by realizing that you are the author."

Mark Houlahan

"Everyone has talent. What is rare is the courage to follow that 'talent' to the dark place where it leads."

Erica Jong

"Live as if you were going to die tomorrow. Learn as if you were to live forever."

Mahatma Ghandi

"Creating a life that reflects your values and satisfies your soul is a rare achievement. In a culture that relentlessly promotes avarice and excess as the good life, a person happy doing his own work is usually considered an eccentric, if not a subversive...To invent your own life's meaning is not easy, but it's still allowed, and I think you'll be happier for the trouble."

Bill Watterson, *Calvin & Hobbes* cartoonist, Kenyon College address, 1990

Loneliness is the poverty of self; solitude is the richness of self."

May Sarton

This is relating to Henrietta Myers "Peter" Miller and a group of art-minded women, many of whom shared a passion for the American Southwest, and all whom evolved far beyond the scope of their roots. Her home town, Hanover, PA, had an unusual history of artists and circles of friends. Many of these were contemporaries and related by both blood and circumstances. Some were much younger, but kept their accomplishments in the local collective memory. Ann Roth, Oscar-winning costume designer, and Rita Mae Brown, prolific author and activist, are two outstanding women from this place.

The aura of these women became a myth for the local underground art-network. Rita Mae Brown excels at writing about mixed messages and highly varied opinions, with hilarious stereotypes and descriptions. Home can be open to both satire and celebration. While there are more connections with fame, lessons, collections, universities, and experiences, we find that we can be "from" a place, yet not "of" that place.

Neighbor and lawyer Jeffrey Valocchi remembers being impressed with "the greatest respect and love for Peter" held by Anne d'Harnoncourt, director of the Philadelphia Museum of Art. She and her husband, Joe Rishel, who still works as Curator of European Paintings for P.M.A., spent quite a lot of time with Peter and her husband Earle. Ted Richardson, former director of the Detroit Museum and creator of the Archives of American Art, and his wife Constance, another serious painter, were part of their circle. Joe tells of delightful lunch conversations and generous loans of art, but also speaks of the aura of people living their philosophy, creating their art.

 Liz Osborne, well-respected contemporary Philadelphia artist, had a close friendship with Peter Miller, those same later years in Philadelphia. She, too, remembers how Peter's life spanned exciting and critical changes in the art world and American art. Her steadfast enthusiasm helped make this book happen.

Another emphasis will be upon the kind of encouragement that was the legacy of these women artists, as well as their bonds in nature and a connected spirituality. I was deeply inspired by them all, and it will be an honor to tell their combined, often convoluted story. I hope that this book will be, in turn, an inspiration for the next generations of artistic souls in small towns, and perhaps a revelation to those who are living in the

4

larger world. Art is a connection that surpasses social differences. The circle only widens.

Call it the Culture Wars - the premise that we must live in any certain urban or national environment to succeed or to excel in the arts, or even to appreciate the same. Yet, this is even more questionable, now in the world of Internet...as well, much of the old middle-class social conditioning (that so many of us endured) is evolving more rapidly. Stereotypes are so boring. Yes, I am playing hardball, here. Women painters with families - impossible? Serious collectors and art in small towns - impossible? Artists, married and remaining so - impossible? Merriam-Webster calls Impossible "incapable of being...or felt to be incapable of being done, attained or fulfilled." Never say never. Peter Miller would like that.

My life and so many others' lives have been staked upon the need to re-define women in the arts, our lifestyles and our choices. Everything is interconnected, yet so many do not see or experience the delightful possibilities. Let me show you some ways the creative spirit evolves and is reinforced - the stories and people who began in a distinctive, and yet common little town, Hanover, PA but extended so very much further.

And so, dear readers, YES...You can grow up in a small town and keep growing. You can choose to live rural, think global, and be happy. Impossible or not, this does not take away from being a True Artist. We can all think and care and still find energy to create. Women will remind us. The Creative Spirit will conquer all. And creativity IS mankind's greatest asset. Don't forget that.

Ever Onward!   *Andrea Miller Theisson*

Chapter One - "Deliciousness" – of Little Girls, Big Thinkers

To grow up in small-town Hanover was to be self-conscious, especially if one's family is "prominent" and late-Victorian. (Edwardian, really, but the girls always called it Victorian.) Yet, we can understand why Peter Miller had a life-long love affair with Nature. Her home boasted a major arboretum, and then there were the animals. Hanover, nestled in lush South Central Pennsylvania, is full of horse people and dog people, her father being one of the main breeders. In that second decade of the 20th Century, Peter Miller had a hard time finding playmates who enjoyed the same things…climbing trees, books, collecting stones, and building fairy homes of moss and acorns under the trees. Her own mother did not want her to get dirty, when playing with her cousins on the farm in nearby Bachman's Valley, Maryland. She was much younger than her brother, Robert, born eleven years earlier in 1903. They were not terribly close, even though he became a well-known, respected outdoorsman.

Her father finally confided in a co-worker, Joseph Kump, who had an only child, Ruth, the same age, also born in 1913. They both had similarly strange interests! So, it was arranged to get them together.

They never parted. They were both hopeless romantics, wanted to be dancers and poets, and they read ALOT. They made up words and nicknames, and ideas. It was an instant friendship– soul-mates for over 70 years! "Deliciousness" they shared.

Their lives would be vastly different at times, yet they kept constantly in contact, visiting whenever they could, swapping poetry and quotations, referring to their worn out copies of William Blake, and much later, Rolling Thunder. They would find themselves at the Pennsylvania Academy of Art and the School of Hard Knocks. Henrietta Myers would become "Peter"Miller, of Chester County, PA, Hanover, PA, and Espanola, NM, while Ruth Kump would become "Jennifer"Kump Bargelt Chapin of Hanover, PA, Colorado, Utah, Wild Horse Mesa, and again, Hanover, PA.

Ruth Kump, thinking *

"Lizzie" Ruth Kump, behind Frederick St., Hanover, PA

They would walk barefoot in creeks, hike, pick up stones, picnic, and have campfires all of their lives. Peter had a penchant for swimming naked – she often said that wearing a suit was "like playing the piano wearing gloves." Jennifer would get that mysterious, squinty-eyed-Western-woman look and stare off cryptically into the distance,

"Kumpie" and "Etts" circa 1930

Ruth Kump, Ethel and C.N. Myers, and "Ettie", circa 1928
All photos this page courtesy of Christa McInturff

then go into a wild tale of exploring the desert with Peter, or just pull out her baskets of stones. Both Peter and Jennifer maintained a spirituality that was a blend of Native American and their childhood Christianity, later becoming more agnostic, and eventually exploring Buddhism, which has parallels to the non-selfish Tewa* paradigm. They learned to dowse. They danced. They celebrated the seasons. They both kept baskets of found objects, small altars to household and nature gods. They reached out to others, swapped books, and encouraged thoughtful conversations. They were both artists, and kept journals. The real stuff of life was their religion – friendship, laughter, love.

"Kumpie" &" Etts" circa 1931

Peter and Jennifer were classmates at Hanover Senior High School, and their 1931 senior yearbook, the *Nornir*, records much of their teen life. They were quite notorious, even then. Both were Latin prodigies, officers in the Literary Society, on the *Orange and Black* newspaper staff, and into the Shakespearean Society, Dramatics and Dance. Jennifer wrote witty comic-relief for the yearbook, Henrietta did half the artwork for the publication. It was the Depression years, and the *Nornir* was a modest book, but full of their spirit. Jennifer "Kump...X – her sign" was noted for being in the Boys Glee Club, while "Ettie," as Henrietta was known then, was listed as "most talented" and for her extensive extracurricular activities, "stunning" prom decorations, and especially two years as a Thalian -"at least 23 months of which must have been devoted to helping devise the horrible initiation ceremony for the 1930 members." This club was dedicated to Thalia, the classical Muse of comedy and idyllic poetry, perfect for these friends!

Peter had many, many stories, and her letters, along with those written to her, are featured in Patrick Burns' book*, *In the Shadow of Los Alamos,* about her chosen godmother, Edith Warner. Edith and Tilano became Peter's godparents just before she was married, being matched up by family friends, possibly John and Martha Boyd, who were Edith's first employers, and neighbors. Edith and Tilano kept the store, guesthouse, and tearoom at Otowi Bridge, right through the years when Los Alamos or "The Hill" became the WWII secret facility for American physicists. Edith Warner was a mystical, magical influence on everyone. Peter and her friends visited many times, especially Jennifer. And they thought about it all...native spirits to physics to politics! This area of New Mexico was truly a power center for many, on many levels!

Black Mesa, San Ildefonso Pueblo, New Mexico.   San Ildefonso Pueblo was founded circa 1300, just south of Los Alamos at present-day Bandelier, then moved to the base of the Mesa near the Rio Grande after a time of lengthy drought. photograph by Ellen Mancini, Santa Fe, NM

Peter's family had taken vacations to New Mexico when she was young. She always felt such a familiarity with the people and the land that they recognized her, as she did their landmarks. The First Americans even "falling down before her" as Jim Schuman said, curator at the Hanover Historical Society's Myers Mansion. Long-time family retainer, Mary Butt, also related the same memory. The curious Myers family had taken Peter to a hypnotist, whose past-life regression told them that she had been a native princess back in ancient times. Later, her work would reflect many mystical images, hard to explain other than some deep connection to the mythology of the Tewa, and earlier Anasazi peoples.

Peter Miller left the role of "Big Fish in Small Pond" to become a small fish in the grand experience of the art world. She never worried about making a living at her art, but she wanted to be acknowledged for her own work, which was dedicated and prolific. Her Pennsylvania Academy application essay on why she wanted to study art reads as her life's testimony:

PURPOSE IN STUDYING ART

Why are you studying art? Because I would rather paint than do anything else

What use do you expect to make of it? No financial use. Simply for my own satisfaction

In your own handwriting and of your own composition, write about your aims and aspirations

To say that I want to study art simply because I love it, seems both sentimental and inadequate, but I can give no other reason. To be constantly aware of loveliness of lines and color, and at the same time, to know that awareness is not enough, and that expression must follow, lead inevitably toward art. I am not studying art with any view of making a living by it, but only because I want to do it so much that I would rather fail at painting than succeed at anything else.

She was privileged in many ways, and went on to a life of comfort and fascinating associations, yet the same as everyone's lives – full of ups and downs. Traveling extensively, Peter spent time in pre-war Paris, meeting both Henri and Pierre Matisse, Hemingway, Max Ernst and many others. This is also the crowd with whom she would have come into contact through Julien Levy, her gallerist in NYC, along with Gertrude Stein and other American ex-patriots. Back in the States, her contacts were just as stellar in the Art World, but she remained who she was…herself! Peter collected people and art, while Jennifer, her best friend, collected stones and rocks. Peter loved the name "Peter" because it means rock in Greek. Jennifer always said that a childhood friend Larry Dawson gave them these names. Mary Butt felt "Peter" was "art-related." Henrietta was going to be her own person, so the name change was fitting.

Chapter Two – The Box

The "late Victorian" years of Hanover, PA were quite typical of many small Eastern towns. The early development had been that of a crossroads, and led to the nickname of "Rogue's Harbor." Hanover is a border town that had agrarian roots, but also some intrigues from smugglers and travelers coming from Baltimore and Philadelphia. The staid German farmers were enlivened by a Scotch/Irish element, many of whom were recruited for their Indian-fighting potential in the early 1700's. William Penn's original land grants remained in families, and the farms prospered, along with mills and tanneries, breweries, cigar factories, and craftsmen. Hanover had its very own Civil War cavalry (of course) battle, and also sheltered some Underground Railroad stops. One of those was right on the Mason-Dixon Line, a farm owned by the Myers family. Peter later inherited this farm, known as "the Sherman farm" after her mother died.* There was a sense of history and entitlement for these old families that continued straight through the 20th Century. Industrialism grew right on history's schedule, and Clinton Noah Myers (1876-1954) was ready.

His friendship with Harper D. Sheppard (1868-1951) and sponsorship by his wealthy father, John Wesley Myers, a Maryland businessman, led to the purchase of the old Heiser Shoe Co. in 1899, which became the Hanover Shoe Co. It was excellent timing to go into the shoe business. Their driving concept was direct sales, and franchised stores everywhere. "CN" and "Shep" built an empire, and Hanover became a company town. The two subsidized many local institutions like the Hanover General Hospital, the public schools, and the public water company; built matching mansions in 1911 and 1912, and actively managed their factory. There was a newsy company paper, full of photos and family stories, with much to connect the workers. The benevolent management impressions were genuinely reinforced. C.N. Myers founded the local newspaper, the Evening Sun, along with Everybody's Poultry Magazine, and was president of the First National Bank.

Other local families including the H.E.Young family and many earlier contributors* built The Hanover Public Library, which opened in 1911, a memorial to young Edward Etzler Young. This was the main cultural edifice of the town, while many social opportunities provided dramatics and music. Yet, the visual art scene in the town was rather bleak, although many were aware of the museums and schools in Philadelphia, and soon, in Baltimore. A few well-educated local ladies, and one of the nuns at St. Joseph's Academy nearby, taught private art lessons. One of these local artists in the 1920's was Bertha Zeiber, in her little house on York St., whose work is still displayed in the now-called Guthrie-Hanover Public Library. Most who desired more sophisticated art instruction had to find mentors in neighboring colleges, private schools, cities.

The Sheppard-Myers coalition displaced several old Hanover businesses, economically and socially. They overshadowed the YMCA with their own Boys Club, providing food, exercise equipment, and showers for young men of the town. Eventually, the Young family's grain mill and brewery lost out to the Shoe Factory for employees and local focus. The Sheppard-Myers partners built an Impounding Dam and park-like grounds, planting a huge watershed with pine trees. And, partly for fun, but with breeding and investment in mind, "CN" and "Shep" founded the Hanover Shoe Farms for Standardbred trotters. It remains one of the most impressive and venerable facilities in harness racing history.*

HANOVER SHOE NEWS   SEVEN

Scene at the Hanover Fair Grounds when the yearlings were shown. Rhea Hanover, bay filly, by Calumet Chuck-Sonya, is being led. Seated at the left with two out-of-town horsemen is Mr. C. N. Myers looking them over.   Photograph Taken By Walter Moore

Hanover Shoe Farms
Yearlings Bring Good
Prices At Auction

pany at the State Farm Show Arena, held in Harrisburg, Nov. 9-11, the eighty-four yearlings offered by the Hanover Shoe Farms brought a total of $94,350, or an average of $1,122. This is the largest number of

1946 Hanover Shoe News

Courtesy of the Hanover Area Historical Society;
Yellen Research Library

The young of the town grew up aware of beautiful horses, with fairgrounds, racetrack, and the show farm just a few blocks from the center square, along with the enormous farms complex a few miles west of town. Clinton Myers also raised and bred his own Blue Bar Kennels English setters, champion hunting dogs. He became passionate about trees*, as well, and had promised his wife an arboretum for a birthday gift, shortly after their mansion on Baltimore Street was built. He took an abandoned, unsightly dump at the next-door brickyard and transformed it into a magical tree park, expanding their side gardens. The property was expanded several times to accommodate the growing gardens and arboretum. Henrietta could see the trees from her bedroom window in town. Later, he did the same at his property adjoining the main Hanover Shoe Farms, which later became the home of young Bob, Henrietta's brother. It remains a beautiful stretch of park-like land, nestled between the pastures of the largest harness horse breeding farm in North America.

Bob always called Henrietta "Etts" which stuck with her through school years. Peter "idolized" her father, later writing a memoir* about his "bigness in heart and mind." C.N., like Peter, would be remembered for many acts of philanthropy and kindness, most of which were not public. Her mother also helped, funding college for many locals. Hanover always had a deeply ingrained sense of filial responsibility and a huge work ethic. Her secretary, Mary Butt Coleson recalls that Peter's mother was different than her father. Henrietta, "Etts", "Ettie" would do the right thing, spending time with her mother biweekly for 25 years after C.N. died in 1954.

Growing up in Hanover was truly like the proverbial fish bowl…and those previously-mentioned big fish in the small pond analogies. Everyone was aware of what others did, and especially so for the privileged families. And everyone watched, judged, and commented upon the young people. It was a difficult place to grow up, terribly inhibiting if you were a creative introvert. Rita Mae Brown absolutely nailed it with her early book *Six of One*, a riotous tale of two sisters in a town that sure sounds like Hanover. We won't even begin to comment on the conservative politics or religious views, but allow that they were classic of the times, and, despite many exceptions, continue to this day as the status quo.

> "Everyday stories are the teaching myths that will show us how to live with each other in our families and towns, how to know what we really want, how to recognize life's enduring pleasures, how to find peace."
> Elizabeth Lesser

Families merged and grew. The friendships and marriages between old families led to many adventures and business agreements, as is usually the way in small towns. Harry Hoffman (1895-1983) moved to town from the farm with his family just before the turn of the century. His father built houses. Quite a few early 1900's Hanover homes show William's style of tightly-laid, dark-mortared brickwork, many on York St.

Harry helped build with his father many years, but he and his best friend Luke Rohrbaugh felt a wanderlust, and took off for California in 1913-1915. They worked their way West, built sheds in Los Angeles, then headed back through St.Louis, where they stopped to get formal portraits photographed, and Harry bought his first motorcycle, an Indian.

They returned to Hanover to settle down with their sweethearts and start families, to develop prosperous lives of entrepreneurship. Harry would eventually own a great deal of downtown Hanover, and some prime out-lying real estate. But they never lost their urge to travel, instilling this in their own children , along with curiosity about the world of Nature, and the West.

photos courtesy of the author and Rohrbaugh family

Harry built a big brick house, just a block or so out Frederick Street from Joseph Kump's 18th Century family home. As "Petie" Miller grew up playing under the trees, eventually joined by "Kumpie" or "Lizzie" as Peter called her, those four Hoffman girls, from the same solid neighborhood, followed, loving nature and the woods. The large Carver family, in the same block as the Kumps, also had a "tomboy"- Charlotte or "Sivvy". She grew close to the girls as well. As a kindred soul, "Siv" or joined them in many pursuits throughout their growing years. Sivvy went on to become an award-winning English teacher in the local schools.

Philadelphia was always considered the more "cultured" of the cities within driving distance (sorry, Bal'more!) back in the day. The City of Brotherly Love had evolved quite an arts scene by the turn of the century. The Pennsylvania Academy was the oldest art school and museum in the country, having been founded in 1805. Comparatively, the Smithsonian Institution (1846) was a newbie. The Wyeths were already an established art dynasty when Peter Miller was born. The Cone sisters would eventually get Baltimore on track with salons and museums, but Philadelphia was more prominently known for culture. Most families of means sent their artistic offspring to Philadelphia, to the Academy, usually after a stint at a "finishing school" or prep school. It was considered a genteel atmosphere in the early part of the 20th Century, and of course, a Grand tour of Europe was also required to round out the education of young aristocrats. Peter was the poster child for a good education.

While Sheppard and Myers both sent their children to public schools, testimony to the quality they subsidized, the alternative was to send the "society" youth to Ivy League prep schools. Peter's family sent her to the "finishing" option after high school. Then, private art lessons with the esteemed Daniel Garber of the New Hope School, a conservative Philadelphia icon. Yet, the beginnings of change were just being felt, as many Pennsylvania Academy of Art grads returned from a Europe full of innovative thoughts. The 1920's and '30's would birth an avalanche of Modernism, Surrealism, Abstraction. Enter Peter Miller, art student. Hold that thought!

Chapter Three - "New Mexico-itis" and "Westering"

Going West. Ah, the challenge of this is pure Americana, from Lewis & Clark to the pioneers to the Teddy Roosevelt - John Muir years. It is Walt Whitman, Wordsworth, and Romanticism, it is economic adventure and gold. It is perhaps finding roots in Nature, pure Nature, that was beginning to be lost to Industrialism by the time our artists were born. Peter Miller was taken to the American Southwest for family vacations. The Sheppards of Hanover sent their son, Lawrence ("LB"), to work as a wrangler on a ranch for two summers before he finished school.

Teddy Roosevelt* spent years out in the Rockies, recovering after losing his first wife. He challenged himself, as a "soft" Easterner, to prove his toughness. As early as the late 1800's, art colonies were beginning to develop in Santa Fe and Taos, as well as many Eastern woodlands. This followed the development of inner city parks in the cities of the East, and the beginnings of an environmental awareness. All these movements – conservation awareness and the glory of the western lifestyle were a backlash of the Industrial Age. (which is a huge generalization, and material for another book)

Peter Miller had felt an instant affinity to the Southwest culture and landscape. Harry Hoffman always felt a kinship there. His daughters and grand-daughters knew it as well. I, his grand-daughter, grew up with cowboy and Indian wallpaper and Taos Society of Arts portraits of great chiefs on the wall of our bedroom in Hanover. There was also one major month-long family vacation, driving through the West, transformative for me! While Mother and Dad debated seeing Mesa Verde over rodeos, we all saw bullfights in Mexico and snow on the mountains in July. Aunt Trudi had horned toads and cacti in aquariums, and sand paintings on the walls, in her Pennsylvania farmhouse. Her sons and daughters all went West, to explore and/or to live for awhile, although all returned to the East. Another branch of the family, Aunt Peg's, moved full-tilt out West, and stayed. The lifestyle of the extended Hoffman family remains one that Peter Miller would recognize. Her best friend Jennifer was part of it all. We gathered around campfires and told stories. We still do.

The world was tuned-into the West. Mabel Dodge Luhan had discovered Taos, and brought her circle of friends there. Others discovered an antidote to harsh cities of the East, and relief from the expenses of living during the Depression era. But there was a huge psychology to this fascination. Why did so many artists of this era find their Muse in New Mexico? Henriette Wyeth married Peter Hurd of NM, a student of her father N.C. Wyeth, but Georgia O'Keefe, Andrew Dasburg, D.H. Lawrence, Robert Henri, John Sloan, etc. moved for art motives- many were Americans from Philadelphia area and New York, quite a few were from the Old World.

"I am, myself, at heart, as much a Westerner as an Easterner." T.D. Roosevelt

Many were there for their health, it being significant how many tubercular artists there were those days. Often those in delicate health were allowed to nurture their creativity in ways that more robust children or young adults could not. Europe was closed off by wars, and many emigrant-artists landed in NYC, where some thrived on city-culture. But, idealistically, a new order of modernism was fascinated by the light and space of the West. What is this but expansive thoughts inspired by, or requiring, an expansive landscape?

Edith Warner, from the Philadelphia area, who had a breakdown* and moved for her health in the early 1920's, and then permanently at age 29, discovered the true connections of her life. Peggy Pond Church's father founded the Pajarito Club, which lasted from 1913-1916, then it became the Los Alamos Ranch School in 1917. Their entire family converted to loving the mesa lands.
Just as Peter Miller and Jennifer were maturing, Santa Fe

> I am glad that the years of adjustment are over, and that there has come to me this new relationship with all of earth. I know that I was never so aware of the river and the trees, that I never walked looking so eagerly for the new wild things growing. I know that I have had to grow sufficiently – no, to cast off enough of civilization's shackles, so that the earth-spirit could reach me.
>
> Edith Warner's journal:
> June 25, 1933
> Reprinted from *In the Shadow of Los Alamos*, with permission from Patrick Burns

was growing into a real artist's colony, with Canyon Road and the El Farol flamenco bar at the high end. Santa Fe would eventually become one of the largest art colonies in the world.

Edith's story is quite fascinating, and has been told many times. Authors Peggy Pond Church, Frank Waters, and Patrick Burns, along with many personal accounts of Los Alamos during the WWII years have gone into much detail. Her connections with Peter Miller and Philadelphia are not quite as clear. Edith was born and raised in the Philadelphia area, the oldest daughter of a Baptist minister, although she has also been described as a Quaker. Quite intelligent and well-schooled, she tried to fit into the East Coast parameters, but found teaching English in Philadelphia "incongenial" and being a secretary for the Easton YWCA too limited. There were health problems, and she went West in 1922 to recuperate and to seek employment, being recommended to John and Martha Boyd's Ranch in Frijoles Canyon, where she worked as a governess and which is now part of Bandelier National Monument. Thwarted romances (there was a cowboy also named Peter) and many health improvements later, she returned to Santa Fe, determined to live there, staying at the La Fonda.

A.J. Connell of the Ranch School linked her up with an opportunity to manage the Otowi Station, a small outpost for deliveries and occasional visitors on the Chili Line railroad that follows the Rio Grande River, at the San Ildefonso Indian Reservation. The Los Alamos Boys Ranch School had been founded just over the ridge, and there was a need to keep the railroad outpost occupied. Edith was an independent soul who loved the solitude of the area. Nature spoke to her. She loved the zen-like quiet of the desert. So, she took a chance.

"Otowi" (OH-tow-wa) means "the place where the water makes noise." Edith wrote many published articles,* mentioned in *The WPA Guide to 1930's New Mexico*. She managed a small tearoom to enhance her subsistence income. Atilano Montoya, a widower and elder of the Pueblo showed up to help, and never quite left. Her access (via Tilano) and understanding of the Pueblo were a great part of her adapted spirituality, which she and Tilano shared with Peter and Earle. Note that Patrick Burns' compilation of Edith's writings, Peter's letters, and their photographs are the ultimate illustrations of this part of Peter Miller's history. The photos, which are part of a collection given to him, are featured in his book, *In the Shadow of Los Alamos, Selected Writings of Edith Warner*. A great deal of this content has to do with Peter Miller, including rare photographs of her, Edith and Tilano. I chose not to duplicate efforts, here, but highly recommend this bridge to the two worlds of San Ildefonso and the Eastern artists and physicists who gathered near Los Alamos, NM.

The Tewa* originally settled this area around 9500 BC, quite a heritage. One family, the Montoyas, had farmed a big spring-fed garden under To-tavi Mesa for generations. And Atilano Montoya, an elder of the San Ildefonso Pueblo, of the same Keres speaking people, was a fascinating character. He joined Edith originally to help with some construction, a much-needed fireplace in 1928, when she first moved into the frame station house. Out of a concern and love for this Anglo woman who lived uncommonly (for the natives) alone bordering their reservation, he lived the rest of his days there.

Tilano amazed Edith by disclosing that he had been to Paris, and knew Philadelphia from when he returned from Europe in 1908. Philadelphia? Europe? She was impressed with his tales of travel with Bostock, the animal trainer-wild west showman, who recruited him and four others from the Pueblo , when they were dancing to show their "novel" culture on Coney Island. They danced the Eagle Dance and worked all over the cities of Europe, but he liked Paris best.

> "Painting is a love affair with the world around you."
> Dorothy Eugenie Brett, Taos painter

The stepped sides of the fireplace that Tilano built would hold the blackware pottery of his family, especially his niece Maria's branch, which Edith hoped to sell to the tourists. This technique was just being revived by Maria Martinez around 1917., and helped establish the art and tourist trade for the Pueblo. The Boyds brought Robert Henri and John Sloan to Edith's tearoom early in her residency, where they shared strawberries from Tilano's garden.

 Edith saw what the artists saw, but her medium was words. In the same journal, Edith wrote of Henri "putting on canvas old Diegito of San Ildefonso and his drum." She would know that family through three generations, in her timeless sense of belonging to this land of "mañana."

The Art Part, Western

As Europe descended into the war years, American artists who had been gathering in Paris came home and began to discover the West. Adolph Bandelier, a Swiss anthropologist, had begun to do a survey of the ruins in the Pajarito plateau and Frijoles Canyon in the year 1880. One of his employees was Julian Martinez of the San Ildefonso Pueblo, along with others.

Bandelier wrote a fiction novel in 1890, *The Delight Makers**, that portrays many of his understandings about the Pueblo culture. This predicted and exemplified that the first Pueblo visitors appreciated the culture as exotic, but ultimately found a deeper interpretation. America was

> "a painter called to language"
> from Carolyn Burke's *Becoming Modern: The Life of Mina Loy*
>
> "Art is language"
> Dennis Akin, painter

looking for something uniquely theirs – an authenticism lacking in the contemporary art of the early 20th Century. The elemental, physical nature of the Southwestern culture became one answer. Bandelier translated.

N.C.Wyeth's "A Sheepherder of the Southwest" appeared in Scribner's, January of 1909. Americans were charmed and curious. This image spoke to our need for frontiers and open space. Even inner cities were developing parks these years, and art colonies were part of the general movement to find natural spaces, and the beauty provided within. By the late 1800's, there were the Catskills and the old Hudson Valley, but Santa Fe and Taos were to be next. While many Pennsylvania Academy of Fine Arts and NYC artists had gone to Paris and Europe looking for Culture, they spent a lot of time together, reinforcing their American identity. From Peter Miller's school, P.A.F.A., went John Sloan, John Marin, and Robert Henri. Marsden

Hartley, Ernest Blumenschein, and Andrew Dasburg (born in Paris, but educated in the US) went to Paris from the Art Students League in New York. They all met Matisse, Leo and Gertrude Stein , Picasso, Kandinsky, Franz Marc, and others from the *Blaue Reiter* School of painters. Peter's animals relate to Klee's. These were the first Modernists, of whatever "school." They were breaking all the rules, finding their way, philosophizing together.

Mabel Ganson Evans Dodge Sterne, patron of the arts and free-spirit collector of art and husbands, had lived in France from 1905-1912 and migrated back and forth through multiple marriages, then finally west to Taos, NM in 1919. Where she married Tony Luhan and "went native." The Taos Society of Artists was quite a realists' unit from 1915-1927, including Joseph Henry Sharp, Ernest L. Blumenschein, W. Herbert Dunton, E.I. Couse, Bert G. Phillips, Oscar E. Berninghaus. Burt and Elizabeth Harwood moved to Taos from France in 1916, and the Harwood Foundation became an entity upon his death in 1923, now a major art museum. Georgia O'Keefe also visited Mabel in 1916. Dasburg was also one of the first to form a major attachment to the Southwest, having visited Mabel in 1918, spending many yearly visits until he moved permanently in 1933.* D.H. Lawrence and Frieda arrived in 1922. Carl Jung visited Taos in 1925. The La Fonda Hotel in Santa Fe, built in 1920, expanded and remodeled extensively in 1929. Walter Ufer's "the Callers" was bought by the National Museum of American Art in 1926. Dorothy Brett arrived in NM in 1924, and 1926 to stay.

Many of the early 20th Century New Mexican artists were representational, and the Taos Society was known to be a bit more academic than some of the Santa Fe crowd. But part of this was the need to make a living as seen in the evolution of the *"Cinco Pintores"*, one of the artists fraternities in the 1920's, who began experimentally and "quickly became more conventional" according to Joe Traugott, curator at the New Mexico Museum of Art.

The symbolic heritage and traditions of 14,000 years of native art would "out" and affect work of prominent painters as well as the lesser known such as Peter Miller. Millicent Rogers moved to Taos in 1940, and her advocacy and museum are legendary. Images and writings about dreams would all predict the trends to the abstraction and Magical Realism of which Peter became a part. Her first solo show at the Levy Gallery was titled *"Incantation."*

Chapter Four - Olé!- Out of the Box!

Peter Miller was sent to the Arlington School in Virginia and then took private art lessons from Daniel Garber (1880-1958), of the New Hope School of painters. He was an American Impressionist, trained 3 years in Europe, who taught at the Pennsylvania Academy after starting in 1907 at the Philadelphia School of Design for Women. He specialized in *plein air* landscapes of Bucks County, often teaching from his home in Lumberville, PA, just north of the city. In 1932, she applied to the Pennsylvania Academy of Art, Philadelphia. There was a rich tradition of classical fine art training here. But the art world was changing fast.

Peter started at the Academy, staying with friends of the family. They introduced her to Earle Miller. Both studied with noted colorist Arthur Carles (1882-1952) who taught at the Academy from 1917-1925, then privately in a "country art workshop" near Brandywine, Chester County, PA. One of Carles' claims to fame was as a major link between Philadelphia and Paris.

Carles was a friend of painter John Marin and photography-pioneer Edward Steichen, and they all were hanging out in Paris from 1907-1910, with the Steins, Leo and Gertrude, and the rest of the American ex-pats. This is where he met Henri Matisse. He showed his own work at the Steiglitz Gallery in NYC from 1910-1912. Carles was known for organizing the first landmark exhibit of Post-Impressionists in Philadelphia with Cezanne and Gauguin, Picasso and Matisse, and an introduction by Leopold Stokowski in 1920, as well as the 1921 show featuring almost 100 American modernists, titled *Later Tendencies in Art*. The second exhibit included Joseph Stella, Marsden Hartley, John Marin, and others. Carles' selections were labeled "crazy extremist" art by conservative critics of the day. One of his biggest supporters and friends at this time was Alfred Barnes*, the collector. Note that both Hartley and Marin, of PAFA, ended up painting in New Mexico after spending a few years in Paris, meeting the same Post-Impressionist crowd. And they were all aware of each other!

Well, Henrietta became "Peter" and she fell for "Pearlie", Charles Earle Miller of Chester County. We do not know much about Earle, other than that he was born in Philadelphia, from an old family in the area, and did not like to be photographed. He wrote of an ancestor buried at Ephrata Cloisters in Pennsylvania, and how he loved that place. There are records of many Irish Quaker families named Miller in Chester County. (Trust me, its like "Smith"...hard to trace anyone.) He did not have any siblings, according to friends. Peter's parents did not quite approve, and it was reported that Earle was not allowed at their home until after Ethel Myers died.

Peter by Earle, untitled, circa 1935
Photography by Andrea Miller Theisson.
Courtesy of
the Brandywine River Museum of Art

Life was fascinating and full. Peter missed a lot of classes, "attendance irregular" and "considerable absences" noted in her student record, but somehow got through the coursework at the Academy. Sort of. She did excel at Construction and Still Life classes. There is a record of her traveling to Europe, most likely her 21st Birthday gift, leaving Europe in 1934 on the ship *Vulcania* from Trieste, Italy to return home. What a good excuse to skip classes! Peter's indomitable spirit of living outside convention is evident here.

"To live is the rarest thing in the world. Most people just exist."
Oscar Wilde

By spring of 1935, Peter was introduced to Edith Warner, the Phila.-born writer who lived at Otowi Bridge outside Santa Fe. Peggy Pond Church wrote "in a roundabout way" Peter came to s stay with Edith "for two months of reflection." Earle then joined her. Peter and Earle were married in a special private ceremony by the edge of the Rio Grande, by Tilano, as a Pueblo official. Edith was their only witness. Of course, there was a "proper"

17

marriage ceremony a few months later, recorded on July 31, 1935 in the Episcopal/Methodist church parsonage in Santa Fe. This one could be formally announced by the Myers family in the

Hanover newspaper. Earle's address was already Santa Fe, probably at the La Fonda. Soon, they built a house at Tunyo, next to the San Ildefonso Reservation. This idyllic beginning was just before the outside world changed.

Peter by Earle, watercolor, circa 1935.
Photography by Andrea Miller Theisson. Courtesy of the Brandywine River Museum of Art

Meanwhile, back to the NY and Paris Art Worlds

Julien Levy, who "discovered" and encouraged so many Modernists and who gave Peter Miller two exclusive solo shows, along with a few group exhibitions, has written a great memoir* of the era, along with records kept in the archives at the Jean & Julien Foundation for the Arts, Inc. - his impressions are first-hand, on target. He loved the "provocative" new art, of all types.*

Julien was a Harvard graduate, with a Fine Arts degree in photography, and a dubious, but wealthy and supportive father. Julien wrote of how Harvard and New York were slowly coming around to receptivity for Modern Art. He was excited about the provocative nature of Surrealists, wanted to "awaken everyone's

Peter Miller at their ranch house 1935.
Ruth Chapin photo
courtesy of Christa McInturff

curiosity and suggest the spirit if not the complete alphabet and poetry of this new tendency in poetry and art. After all, improvisation rather than calculation is much nearer the essence of Surrealism, the 'school of the unconscious.' What is more, I believe that, like a sense of humor, it should be practiced in the most contagious way, daily and by *everyone*."

He was in Paris the first time in 1927-28, a trip arranged with Duchamp on a Surrealist filming excursion. Julien had adopted Marcel Duchamp and Alfred Steiglitz as his "godfathers" in the art business. Duchamp's theory was not to live for profit or loss, but to Live, capital "L," period. Julien met many artists and writers at Gertrude Stein's – Pavel Tchelitchew, Adrienne Monnier, Paul Valery, and Max Jacob, and Adrienne's friend Sylvia Beach, whose bookstore Shakespeare & Co. was where all the American ex-pats hung out. D.H. Lawrence was there often. Julien also met the sculptor Brancusi and Max Ernst on this trip. "This was a heady brew such as one could not hope to find assembled and accessible in New York those days."

Julien Levy had planned to see poet/entrepreneur Mina Loy, whom he had met in NYC with the Steichen/O'Keefe crowd. On his first day there, he met her daughter Joella Loy, along with Isadora Duncan, at a party held by Peggy Guggenheim, then Mrs. Lawrence Vail. He stayed near them through the insistence of Yankee writer/publisher and man-of-the-world Bob McAlmon that he must experience the *quartier* of the artists. Bob "knew everyone of importance in the Arts." Bob was a good friend and patron of William Carlos Williams, Ezra Pound, Marsden Hartley, Ernest Hemingway, and Ford Maddox Ford. I could drop big names all day, but it is important to remember that this is the crowd of Peter Miller. Many had gone to Pennsylvania Academy of Art, or were from the NYC and Philadelphia art worlds, and she would have met them through Julien, and friends, in Europe and the States.

So, Julien and Joella, a beautiful and "competently mature" 19-yr-old, fell in love. With much hesitation on Mina's part, they married. Mina had a very Bohemian lifestyle, and had been already married twice, once to Joella's father, Stephen Haweis, a man of moderate inheritance. They lived in trendy Florence. Then he left for the Bahamas after the children were born. Her second husband was Surrealist poet and prizefighter Craven Lloyd, a nephew of Oscar Wilde. Craven then disappeared in Mexico, presumed dead. She had reasons to doubt marriage. Her family was sponsored pretty much by Peggy Guggenheim, those years. Julien and Loella sailed back to the US in 1931, the same year that Peter Miller graduated from high school.

Julien Levy had his first show of American photography that year, 1931. Along with other big "S" names, Sheeler and Steichen, Alfred Steiglitz was in it, also Man Ray and Lee Miller. Steiglitz had a theory of never signing his work – "When I am asked why I do not sign my photographs, I reply: Is the sky signed? I have always believed that what people give in return for a work of art should be equivalent to what they feel they can sacrifice, in order to free the artist to live, to create further, in freedom…" Peter Miller never signed her work on the front, as didn't Jennifer. They both would have been aware of Steiglitz' philosophy.

In 1934, Julien sailed back to Europe with Joella. A young Peter Miller was leaving on her Grand tour the same year. Perhaps they met on the ship?

This was an eventful trip for Levy, who met Salvador Dali and was immediately impressed with the Dadaists. He became involved in planning an exhibit of Dali's work in NYC, working with Pierre Matisse and Pierre Colle, but feared the customs agents. The art was "questionable." "No fear," said Pierre."Monsieur Dali has promised to make himself unobjectionable. He will modify. Just a little unobjectionable, but enough. He is so versatile." Pierre had three of the new paintings, they were *sans ordure* (not filthy) and certainly masterly and startling enough. 'If not the old Roquefort, at least,' as Dali was to say, the real Camembert.'" Thus, *"The Persistence of Memory"* was bought by Levy, as the other two were already sold.

Levy was surprised when he returned to the apartment in Paris with the painting and found his father visiting. Not by the visit, but "To my surprise Dad was enthusiastic. He commented on the meticulous technique; he took the image to represent the 'flow of time.' This interpretation would not have occurred to me among all the other aesthetic and philosophical implications of that picture. 'Time flies, isn't there a fly on the watch?' he joked." And so *Persistence de la Memoire*" became *The Limp Watches*." This is so like a story that would happen in Hanover, perhaps a version of Peter Miller's tolerant father, CN Myers, viewing a Surreal piece. And the elder Levy saw the investment potential (at $250., the highest they had paid for any one work)!

At this point, Julien notes that his "interests divided between these possibilities; Surrealism, the literal dream world, and Neo-romanticism, the nostalgic world of fantasy." His exhibit of Dali's watercolors and etchings in late spring 1934 and the fall show of "Eight Modes of Paintings- a survey of 20th Century Art" (Monet, Renoir, Matisse, Rousseau, Braque, Picasso, Leger, Otto Dix, Kandinsky, Nolde, Dali, Klee, Ernst, Miró and more) were hugely successful. He considered his discovery of Joseph Cornell his greatest *coup* as a dealer, and regrets only a few omissions from his earliest shows (Miró and Tanguy), but, Levy wrote "the Ernsts, on the other hand were legitimate Surrealism and magnificent."

We know that Peter and Earle Miller knew and socialized with Max Ernst and Dorothea Tanning. She greets them with love in a note to Julien, prior to her second show with the gallery. There is also a postcard written to Peter by sculptress Louise Bourgeois, sending good wishes and a clipping about her show. Bourgeois' husband, the critic Robert Goldwater, wrote "Peter Miller, a young artist exhibiting at the Julien Levy Gallery, experiments tastefully – and sometimes with courageous spirit –in the manner of the Surrealist moderns, of whom Klee is no doubt her favorite…tends to show only how clever Peter Miller is at assimilating the spirit of others." In Art Digest, she is praised for "dream patterns and clever personal use of Indian symbols."

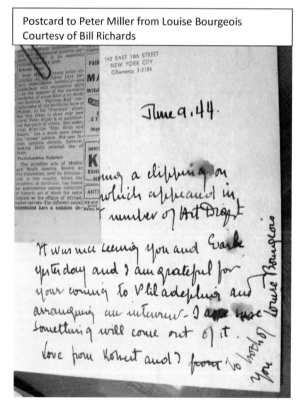

Postcard to Peter Miller from Louise Bourgeois
Courtesy of Bill Richards

Julien made many subsequent buying trips to Paris, until war broke out in full. He often stayed at Mina's apartment, across from Djuna Barnes, in proximity to the artists' *quartiers* of Montparnasse and the Saint-Germain district. "Mina's household, always in a state of delicate equilibrium between threadbare poetic freedom and aristocratic elegance, would be a perfect location for my own balancing act between America and Europe, the new world and the old." No wonder there was a rapport between Peter Miller and this man, albeit her standards of morality were quite a bit less indulgent. Julien went on through many affairs and three wives. The second was painter Muriel Streeter. His third wife, Jean Farley Levy, retired to Taos in 1999.

These years, the newlyweds Peter and Earle Miller were dividing their time between the SW and the Philadelphia/NY art scene. Alex Calder, from the Philadelphia area, briefly organized café dancing on Sunday evenings in a restaurant on upper third Ave. in Greenwich Village. (Millers bought "quite a few" Calders) Their mentor, Arthur Carles was a close friend of John Barrymore, as well as Philadelphia's W.C. Fields. Jennifer told of a story about Peter being

along with a crowd which included John Barrymore, famous actor and a notorious drunk. He was too loaded to remember his lines for one of his last productions, most likely when he was to play Sheridan Whiteside in *The Man Who Came to Dinner* in 1942. He ended up in a hospital, where he told his friends he felt like he "was in an egg." Barrymore had originally studied to be an artist, but his theatrical family genes won out. Dramatic he was!

Peter in the early '40's , Ruth Chapin photo
Courtesy of Christa McInturff

Jeffrey Valocchi tells us, "We loved her stories of being in Paris in the 40's, meeting the likes of the Matisse brothers, Picasso, Miró, and other artists and writers. I was a Lit. major at Notre Dame, so Peter and I would have many conversations about literature and she made it a point, on many occasions to let us know how much she hated Hemingway and his writing. She really didn't consider him an artist/author." Jennifer said that she spoke of all the other big names as "just like normal people."

Meanwhile, Jennifer had gone to Randolph-Macon in Virginia and received a far more practical training. She was in love with a respectable Hanover scion, Louis Bargelt, great grandson of a founding father of the town, and a handsome young soldier.

While Jennifer had traveled west with Peter earlier, and loved it, she chose a more conventional life to begin her adult years – A son, Joe, was born in 1936. Shortly afterward, it was revealed that Louis had contracted a debilitating social disease, and had hidden it for years. A friend from the military (or "school" according to another source) had also contracted the same disease, but had come forth for early treatment and

survived. The evidence was disturbing and Jennifer divorced Louis, a difficult choice, those years. Joe was sent to Mercersburg Academy, helped by Peter. And Jennifer went to work, first as a dental hygienist, as trained, then at a Sears store. She was very proud to support her son alone. She remained quite adamant and would not accept further help, from Peter or anyone.

Above right:Louis Bargelt; left:Joe Bargelt w/Earle's horse Chico
All photos, this page by Ruth Chapin, courtesy of Christa McInturff

Somewhere along these years, as many times earlier, Peter took Jennifer out to visit her godmother in New Mexico. They both felt at home with the mesas and open land, walking far and wide, collecting rocks and shards. Tilano would chastise them for filling their pockets with the "god stones" and he would tell them to return them to the land. Some, however, no doubt "spoke" to the young women and ended up in baskets at home. The ongoing friendship was a respite for Jennifer. And Earle taught Tilano the wolf whistle!

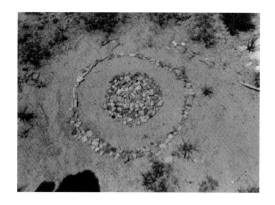

> "During a time when certain stones knew your name, they would be placed in your medicine pouch. These ancestor stones became your guide because they were here first, even before life, and possess ancient knowledge."
> www.Ya-Native.com

untitled Peter Miller painting, gifted to Joe Bargelt

Courtesy of Christa Bargelt McInturff

Petroglyphs above Otowi,

photo by Ruth Chapin
Courtesy of Christa Bargelt McInturff

Peggy Pond Church, future "poet laureate" of NM was also peaking creatively these years. Peggy and Peter were young newlyweds at the same time, but Peggy struggled with raising three boys and a tenuous marriage. Peggy was also a special friend of May Sarton, prolific and successful poet/writer, who often visited New Mexico. Edith Warner became a big fan of Sarton, whom she knew through Peggy, and recommended her books to Peter. Peggy had attended camps and schools in New England, bonding their experiences even more. All of these artists, literary or visual, felt the links with Nature most strongly.

> "All of us who spent any time at the river learned something from Tilano...the knack of letting the funny side of life exist always beside the serious...the same voice that told Peter, as he guided her hand in gesture on the high sacred places 'make your prayer NOW' could also tease us with wolf calls if we appeared in jeans that hugged too tightly." Peggy Pond Church

In 1942, the army commandeered the Los Alamos Ranch School as a remote outpost for their physicists' secret mission. During that era, Edith, Tilano's and Peter's visits were limited because of the war efforts; with both godparents' involved in Pueblo affairs, the demands of supplying garden produce and "entertaining" the physicists with their wives by providing a much-needed sense of normalcy for nights "out", along with national travel restrictions.

Meanwhile, those Hoffman girls were maturing just as all hell broke loose in the world. Their husbands, after an idyllic upbringing and courtships that involved alot of cabins, canoes, and campfires, were off to the war.

Mary, my mother, spent the war years working as a buyer for The Lana Lobell Stores, owned by Boris and Sophie Leavitt, art collectors who had moved from NYC/Philadelphia to Hanover to build a business, raise their children, and show horses. Their farms were not as large as the Hanover Shoe's, but they had quality horses, more thoroughbreds and show horses. Russian immigrants from 1921, who had escaped the wars in their native land, the Leavitts had moved to Hanover in 1934 and had begun to seriously collect art. Boris would take Mary to the Russian Tea Room, the garment district, and then galleries. It was an education that was as good as formal college. Mary also got to ride the excellent horses that Boris kept at his barns in town, just a block away from her home.

Boris collected for investment, but also for the love of art. He owned works by DeKooning, Giacometti, Lichtenstein, Diebenkorn, Andy Warhol, Pollock, Alex Calder, Jean Arp, David Smith, Picasso, Braque, Gris, Philip Guston, and Renoir. I remember playing billiards next to the Renoir nude, swimming next to the Smith, and holding a Faberge salt-cellar, shaped like a monkey, in my hand…and Dead Sea scrolls in a display case! What a great exposure for those of us who knew them!

Their son David, my schoolmate and friend, also married an artist, Gail MacMillan. Boris (1905-1996) and Sophie (1906-1992) retired to Florida in the 1980's. They were gracious and mentoring friends to my mother, and influential Hanoverians, and exposed us all to so much modern art.

Untitled oil painting by Trudi Hollinger
courtesy Carol Hollinger

The oldest Hoffman daughter Trudi, married John DeGuy Hollinger, who had a bad back, so stayed home from the war to buy a farm, develop his family insurance/real estate business, and raise four children. It was a good life, on a big farm, with lots of parties and extended family, horses, cattle, dogs, and cats. Trudi kept her garden, her own version of a blank canvas, and took more painting lessons – often, her sister Mary, went along. They studied under Herb Leopold, a formidable Italian holding classes in York, PA. Both these oldest Hoffman "girls" took art classes from the best in the area – they sought out Othmar Carli, an Austrian master, nearby, and Ernest Krape, with his Cubist style at Gettysburg College . Friend "Flossie" Wolfskill painted along with them, innovating images and portraying Modernist and risqué subjects, perhaps to just keep Hanover on its toes? Most local painters were realists.

> "Gardening is a living poem, a co-creation…my garden, my life, my poems – a planned disorder…whatever we create is made of the materials of the life."
> Stanley Kunitz,
> *The Wild Braid*

Trudi eventually traveled to Greece, Mexico, Guatemala, Florida many, many times then Bermuda and Sanibel for workshops and more art studies. Trudi Hoffman Hollinger inevitably went to Santa Fe and did the desert-artist's tour, including a ride behind a Native American young man on a motorcycle, across the desert. The story, evocative of the famous poster of Georgia O'Keefe, became a family favorite. Yet, she always came back to her old farmhouse and the beautiful garden.

Bob and Ruth Chapin, CO
All photos this page, courtesy of
Christa McInturff

Jennifer had met the love of her life, Bob Chapin, while she was working. They immediately made plans to move West, marrying in 1953. They headed to Colorado, but on a business speculation they moved to Salt Lake City, then back to Colorado. It was heartbreaking for them, newly arrived in Arcata, CO in 1965, when a flashflood destroyed much of the ancient family furniture they had so carefully brought along for their new life. But, it was just "stuff."

They saw a good bit of Peter and Pearlie, as they were closer to each other, and they all went out dancing – square-dancing, flamenco at El Farol, and to bullfights, hiking, picnicking, and roaming the hills.

Betsy and Joe Bargelt and baby
Courtesy of Christa Bargelt McInturff

All was promising. In 1963, Joe had just married Lizbeth Hollinger, daughter of Trudi Hoffman and John Hollinger of Hanover, more old families combined. They would also move to Colorado, have two daughters whom they took camping on skis, backpacking, and taught them to love mountains. Jennifer was a nearby grandmother who taught them about stones and art and dancing. She took her young granddaughters and "goddaughter" Karen Findling's girls along with Peter, to wade barefoot in creeks near Estes Park, and to paint stones with watercolors. Always, they did outdoor, fun things. And it seemed everyone was moving out West.

The Hoffman family kept procreating and celebrating life – the "dirty dozen" grandchildren grew up close and always exposed to the Western myths. One branch, the Littles (Peg's gang) defected to first Illinois, then Colorado in the '60's. Uncle Chick taught architecture at the University of Southern Illinois, and Aunt Peg took up welding sculptures and photography. Their summer home in Cascade, CO. became a magnet for their children, and eventually a retirement home. Trudi's children followed – Betsy and Joe having moved first; then Susan and Ed followed to attempt a pretzel business in CO, where all the transplanted Easterners missed good pretzels. Alas, the water and the wheat and altitude worked against the traditional German pretzels we all loved from PA.

Susan and Ed returned to the East. Betsy and Joe divorced, and not long afterwards, another tragedy happened– Joe 's suicide in 1978. Betsy and her girls moved to Florida. Art school and acting were in the future for these goddaughters of Peter. Peg Hoffman Little's children all went into the arts – Steve was first trumpet in the Navy Band, and a musician all of his life; Gretchen became a painter and art teacher,

Stacey is an artist and graphic designer, while Kari is a dancer , costume designer, and performance artist. Trudi Hoffman Hollinger's granddaughter Carol went into art school, to become a successful graphics designer. Her Aunt Susan picked up a brush those years, too.

All this time, Peter and Jennifer remained dutiful daughters and returned regularly to visit and care for their mothers, both aging comfortably in Hanover. On a few occasions, the older generation from Hanover would come to visit – Ruth Chapin's mother and mother-in-law both made the trip.

"Nana K," Jennifer, and Bob
Chapin's mother, Colorado
courtesy of Christa McInturff

Ethel Myers wrote cordial letters to Edith Warner, and sent gifts, frequently table linens for the tearoom. Peter always sent clothes and food-gifts to Edith and Tilano, who wanted nothing but practical items. Gardens were another link between the families. While Edith and Tilano lived very simply, it is known that Edith did have a few paintings and prints by Peter and Earle, mentioned in letters. Edith listened to the radio broadcasts of symphonies whenever she could. The Santa Fe Opera did a performance of Madame Butterfly, ironically written by John Luther Long of Hanover. Small world! Eventually, the S.F.O. would honor Peggy Pond Church with her poetry put to music.

Karen Findling remembers how there was a different energy to New Mexico than that in Colorado. "Somehow more mystical." The natives believe that this is a vortex or power spot, and the presence of the physicists at Los Alamos perhaps incited some more creative scientific thought. Many of those same physicists fell in love with the land and stayed in the region, keeping an ongoing dialog between the artists and their theories.

Edith's tearoom had been a "refuge for the elite cast of geniuses"* and the theory of light as wave and partical, as part of the same thing, spoke to her understandings of nature. The Pueblos always knew that "harmony in nature consists of interplay of apparently conflicting forces." And so, the reverence for transformations of energy could apply to the locals and to art. Edith Warner wrote of her friendship with Niels Bohr, known as "Nicholas Baker" to the neighbors. Oppenheimer and his wife Kitty knew Edith before the Los Alamos facility was ensconced, and frequented her place all through the war years, along with bringing many friends as a "welcome distraction." Jennet Conant writes about the physicists' love for Edith and her cooking in *109 East Palace: Robert Oppenheimer and the Secret City of Los Alamos*. Ethel

Jennifer, Justine and Henry "Ronny"Laquer, and
Heidi Bargelt on a later visit , circa 1987
photo: Christa McInturff

and Darol Froman became post-war neighbors of Edith's and were helping her at the end of her life. Justine and Henry Laquer were immediate neighbors of Peter and Earle in Espanola.*

"They said 'You have a blue guitar,
You do not play things like they are."

Wallace Stevens

"As an artist, you love everything of quality that came before you.

An artist is valued for his personal interpretive insight and not for his conformity to traditional patterns. So, it is always an indication of uncertain knowledge if, when judging a work of art, one compares the work of one artist with that of another."

Hans Hofmann

of Hofmann: "He is a painter of physical laws with a spiritual intuition."

Tennessee Williams

"It's that a whole era is ended; is totally repudiated, a whole era of brains and literary and excited thinking."

Eric F. Goldman

"Oh, painters are like a big Irish family in the potato famine! There's never enough of anything to go around – collectors, galleries, grants, prizes...but I'm so old now, I've got nothing to lose."

Kate Christensen, *The Great Man*

Contexts and Conflicts in the Art Scene

The context of Peter Miller's life and the mature years of her work are deeply defined by the Modernists and Surrealists, but also the general mid-Century art world. Her friendships and associations are definitive of the caliber of her personality and style. I see her work as exceptionally original, a synthesis of the uniquely American Pueblo culture and the most sophisticated of international art movements.

While Peter and Earle Miller may have chosen to live away from the main action of the New York scene, they certainly were engaged in it enough to keep abreast of the latest ideas and discussions. From the early influence of Arthur Carles and the Philadelphia crowd, the WPA artists and projects, and then the extended "family" of the Julien Levy and Pierre Matisse gallery shows, which includes many of the biggest names in the world of art, Peter Miller was there.

It seemed like the first half of the 1940's was a time of struggle for the American artists to find themselves, to place their work within a wider evolution of art. While these earlier artists, Peter's age and a bit older, had made the world pay attention to the Surreal and the Dadaists' anti-political stance, to dreams and Magical Realism, along with the practical and reflective images of WPA Art, the mid-Century artists were shifting gears. There was much that Peter would relate to, and some that she would distain.

Han Hofmann and others would bring a new energy to NYC and Greenwich Village. It would intensify the pace of artists' evolution into the abstract. Josef Albers had moved up from Black Mountain, an experimental college in North Carolina, bringing Bauhaus sensibilities and a simplification of expression. The increasing prosperity and frenetic pace of America those years was hard for many of the old-school artists to assimilate. Jed Perl writes that Miró complained that he could not live the life he wanted to, "...and with so much going on I become too tired to paint."

Relating to Peter Miller's work and life, Fairfield Porter (1907-1975), who also came from a wealthy family, and whose father was also an avid naturalist and architect, wrote quite a bit about his art and justification for his work. He defined the curves of Jean Arp as "indicative of infinity." Much of Peter's work includes visual reference to how Jean Arp made his "infinite" shapes. A few years later, Donald Judd would write of Arp's efforts as "a sensation of wholeness." These are certainly theories that Peter Miller would have embraced.

Porter also loved Wallace Stevens' poetry. Stevens (1879-1955), who was born in Reading, PA, was a favorite of Peter Miller's as well, with his celebration of the human imagination. His work also had been published in *Broom,* a 1920's magazine featuring many of the American ex-pats and international Paris radicals. Stevens is quoted in the journal that Peter and Jennifer shared.

Jed Perl, in his *New Art City – Manhattan at Mid-Century* landmark compendium of intellectual movements and how they affected artists, writes of Julien Levy's crowd: "While they had all embraced the modern idea that artistic expression was lodged in the bones and muscles of style, they had not gone on to conclude that art should therefore be all bones, all muscles…in fact, they believed the reverse…that the essential unity of artistic expression freed them to appreciate many different styles….the history of art since the late nineteenth century was, in short, a grand collage." Indeed, the "metaphysical melting-pot" was getting stirred.

James Lancel McElhinney, an art scholar and Tyler-Yale grad, has written in an essay about Charles Curran that "The Old Masters built up a tradition that there is first of all such a thing as good composition; that good drawing is not necessarily slavish and stupid imitation of nature; that color and tone…can be treated in a wide variety of manners…and that an understanding of and sympathy with humanity must be his guide as to what beauty is."*

Peter Miller surely enjoyed the late-40's artists' magazine titled *The Tiger's Eye,* with its title borrowed from William Blake. While a limited run, it featured many contemporaries and indigenous art. It combined the Surrealists' "last stand for Neo-Romanticism" with the latest works by painters like Jackson Pollock. His action-painting and interest in American Indians could be determined to be a combination of dance and sand-painting, with floor perspectives. Now that would have got Peter's attention.

And her old friend Max Ernst had a large collection of *kachina* dolls from the Southwest. One can only surmise that they all talked about and shared these things.

In the 1950's, NYC truly came into the spotlight as an art city. It had "arrived" to compete with Europe. It was a "Golden Age" with a glamorous mix of artists, museums, critics, curators, and historians. And, as Jed Perl writes, it was "creepily sentimental." The Cold War instilled a conservative, conforming influence over the country. Artists and writers looked inward for their inspiration, especially during those McCarthy years.

Painted stones, untitled –Peter Miller (l) and Ruth Chapin (r) Courtesy of Christa McInturff

Then by the '60s things were getting wild. Another sea change was in the forecast. Nell Blaine worried about the idea of "novelty above all." Abstract Expressionism had its backlash into classicism, or complete deconstruction. And weren't those early acrylic paints just awful? The job of artists became to show alternate visions of everything. It was refreshing to know that some held fast to a mature, individual style. Peter Miller was one of them.

 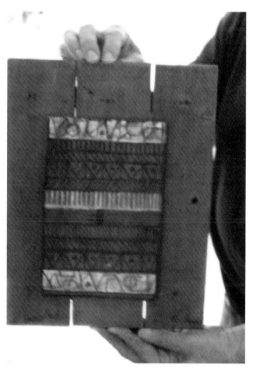

Bill Richards, artist, showing an example of his friend Peter Miller's constructions. Two-sided, it had a stone imbedded in the center of the front. There were many small constructions, reminiscent of Cornell, but always with her own Kachina-like figures or stones and painted petroglyphs.

Photograph by the author   Courtesy of Bill Richards

1.   (at Peter Miller's ranch)

It is terrible to be so moved by a mere stone
On its remnant of riverbank from a past age;
A white stone as round as a kneecap or a child's skull,
Not so much white as mooncolor,
Not so much round as oval;
A marvel of substance, of hardness
That time alone could mold,
Time and the thrust of a long-vanished river,
Torrents of water rolling it over and over
The way we children once rolled clay between our curved palms.

2.

My heart stops to think how stones are always in the making
That seem to lie about so quiet and speechless
In a bed of dry arroyos.
They form patterns like the handfuls of jacks we used to play with,
Sorting themselves into numbers,
Becoming threes, fifteens or sixes,
Playing Still Pond No More Moving
Until the fierce disorder of the next storm frees them
Once more into motion, rolling them on and onward,
Grinding them against one another,
Abrading them with sand grains,
Flinging them loose once more at random
Like a spilled alphabet,
Clusters of words to be read like an oracle.

3.

You said as we started our walk inside the crystal
Of that October afternoon,
"I have always thought this place is really heaven."
So I too found it.
This was the miracle: the two of us were witness
To the same transubstantiation,
The ripplemarks in the sand, the cliff shapes echoed
In the low sandy borders of the arroyo,
The individual beauty of each strewn stone
As thought each contained an angel.

4.

This moon-white stone
Was inscribed along its brow with a cryptic writing
Like a musical notation,
A message that seemed to speak, not to our learning
But to a wisdom in us like the stone's
That we read without knowing how we read.
I grope for words to translate but I cannot.
The meaning is felt, not read.
There is a god in this stone or something like one.
Within us there is something like a god that answers.

5.

Kneeling, we laid our hands on the warm stone and listened,
Touching the stone in a mutual benediction.
Human and mortal as we were, the mute stone blessed us
And absorbed from us our blessing;
Its angle and ours touched hands.
I heard – did you hear? – the sound of an ancient river
And the cry of great birds in migration passing over.
From This Dancing Ground of Sky   permission of Kathleen Church

Chapter Five- Peter's Prime, Late Bloomers, Early Exits

The post-war years flew! Life was good, and sometimes sad – as ever, a mix. The post-war years brought drought and heartbreak to the San Ildefonso reservation and neighbors. Edith Warner died, after a long but graceful decline, in 1951. It was cancer, and we can only speculate about the origins. Her health had never been robust, and years of hard work had taken a toll as well. Peter was there with her at the end, as was Peggy.

Tilano died in 1953, at a much older age, estimated to be "about 80-85."

Back East, more heartbreak…
Peter's father died in the summer of 1954. Her brother, Robert "Bob", died in 1959, a sudden and unexpected heart attack. As a much-respected outdoorsman, conservationist, and sportsman, his own philanthropy went to various nature preservation societies.

But life is a balancing act…
Peggy Pond Church spent a good bit of time with the Millers at their ranch. She wrote several poems at their place. May Sarton also wrote of Tilano and her visits with him and Edith. In her *Letter to An Indian Friend,* she asks "What is the first prayer, Tilano?" There was much interaction between the old friends these years, with Jennifer, Bob, and "goddaughter,"Karen Findling, coming to visit from Colorado. They always did something "off the grid," exploring the desert, hiking.

There is a revealing story that Peter wrote to Edith Warner about when they heard that WWII was over. All their friends just automatically came over to celebrate, and Peter and Earle handed out drinks, going through the motions, but they could hardly wait, as soon as everyone left… to throw down blankets in the grass and look up!

Entrance to Peter and Earle Miller Ranch and the side-yard.
Photograph by Ruth Chapin   courtesy of Christa McInturff

Peter had been showing at many venerable locations by this time, but there became a gap in the shows, with the Levy Gallery closing and family duties. Peter and Earle became more dedicated patrons of the arts. Yet, many friends encouraged shows, and PAFA featured both of the Millers, in several exhibits. Little-known fact: Peter Miller was an avid football fan. Another odd combination – a fine artist who totally enjoys all-American football! Old friend Bob Ingersoll tells us that she rooted for the Miami Dolphins, knowing all the players' names, etc. His daughter, Isobel, was another "goddaughter" of Peter's. Meanwhile, Bill Richards remembers that Peter was an Eagles fan. Perhaps both! There was mention of an infatuation with quarterback Roman Gabriel. So, we know what she did on late fall & winter Saturday or Sunday afternoons.

> "If you can't get rid of the skeleton in your closet, you'd best teach it to dance.
>
> George Bernard Shaw

> "I have perceiv'd that to be with those I like is enough,
> To stop in company with the rest at evening is enough,
> To be surrounded by beautiful, curious, breathing, laughing flesh is enough.
> I do not ask any more delight, I swim in it as in a sea.
> There is SOMETHING in staying close to men and women and looking on them, and in the contact and odor of them, that pleases the soul well,
> All things please the soul, but these please the soul well."
>
> Walt Whitman

Peter and Earle developed a regular routine of spending half the year in the East, at Rock Raymond and Hanover, then migrating back to the ranch in Espanola for the rest of the year. When Peter and Jennifer got together, they still took a picnic and headed for the mountains, the streams, the woods. This was Black Mesa or the 15,000 acres of leased Reservation land in Espanola, or Michaux State Forest in Pennsylvania.

Peter, Peggy Pond Church, and Earle at the ranch   unknown photographer
courtesy Sharon Snyder

Among the Holy Stones
The world I moved through all day
seemed as much inside me
As it did all around.

Shakespeare's "delighted spirit" got mixed
with Blake's bird,
That "vast universe of delight" our senses
Most often keep closed out.

These were
 once fiery New Mexico mountains we
walked on.
Inside, a mountain of transfiguration
became their reflection.

"In your own Bosom you bear your heaven
and Earth and all you behold."

We drank our thermos coffee on a hillside
among the holy stones.

(at Peter's ranch)
Peggy Pond Church, 1965
permission of Kathleen Church

They all loved their music and small gatherings of friends, good conversation, and good thinking. Peter and Earle had dinner parties almost every weekend. Joe Rishel and Ann D'Harnoncourt of the Philadelphia Museum of Art, Liz Osborne of Philadelphia Academy of Fine Art, neighbors Jeffrey and Beth Valocchi, the Goodyears and Wyeths, the artists of the Levy Gallery and the Phila. area.

Bill and Charlene Richards became friends with Peter and Earle in the early '70s, at the gallery where Charlene was director, where they got their framing done in Philadelphia. Bill was teaching at Moore College of Art those years. They became friends and got

Earle, Peter, and Audrey Osborne
Courtesy Elizabeth Osborne

together at the farm about every other weekend, for nearly 20 years. They found support and appreciation in these compatible intellects. Friends became family. Bill remembers that Peter couldn't "play the role as an artist, but they were VERY serious artists" And yet, she was a very fierce competitor at croquet.

While the Millers had bought their first farmhouse in Pennsylvania in 1937, Rock Raymond and 99 acres, they kept adding to the property with small plots in 1940, 1950, 1954, and 1958. Then, in 1961, they bought the adjoining Harkaway Farm, 112 acres and the Hopewell Schoolhouse with 14 more acres in

31

1964. Their holdings in Chester Co. totaled 252.9 acres. Bill remembers Earle as more of a "gentleman farmer and businessman." Both the Millers felt that they could not be taken seriously as artists. Oh, but they could! And, should!

There was a landed-gentry of artists in Chester and Bucks counties in Pennsylvania who raised horses, dogs, and livestock. The families also had many ties to New Mexico, the Brandywine River Museum, Philadelphia Museum of Art, and PAFA. Millers collected Calder, Miró, Nadelman, Gorky, Braque, Horter, and more.

Audrey Osborne on "Buck"
Courtesy of Audrey O. Cooper

Peter, Liz and Audrey at Rock Raymond Farm
Courtesy of Elizabeth Osborne

Jennifer kept collecting rocks. Peter collected people. And they both collected ideas.

Liz Osborne* also re-grouped around that time, spending some time at Peter's guest house on Sosaya Lane in Santa Fe, and much time at the farm, Rock Raymond. Her daughter Audrey became another goddaughter of Peter's, and remembers building the same fairy houses among the tree roots that we all shared with these magical grandmothers. Audrey Osborne Cooper is now an active working ceramic artist. Audrey wrote : "The Millers and Rock Raymond Farm are so dear to me – a hugely influential part of my childhood. Thank you for recognizing their magic." Many other friends' children experienced the blessings of Peter and Jennifer's creative nurturing, advice about art schools, and suggestions. Simple exposure to their collections and little altars of ephemera, shards, stones, and found objects of all descriptions made an impact upon our imaginations. Inspiration!

Philadelphia was still an active market for Peter and Earle. Pennsylvania Academy of Art and the philanthropic, artsy Cosmopolitan Club downtown kept Peter in the network, a "good group" according to Liz Osborne. Earle was on the board at P.A.F.A. and working with the Philadelphia Art Alliance. They both had shows, together and separately in Philadelphia. (see exhibitions) They collected more – "Slumber" serigraph by Morris Blackburn, a litho of Wallace Stevens poem "Blackbirds," graphically rendered by Dennis Umholtz.

Memory of Mykonos, Trudi Hollinger   Courtesy of Carol Hollinger

Trudi and Mary Hoffman kept taking classes and raising their kids, developing amazing gardens that reflected artistic sensibilities...lush, colorful palettes, choreographed for color through the seasons. They both developed into couture-level seamstresses, and got into hat-making – a typical vacation was a trip to the Garment District in NYC for supplies and fabrics. Trudi "had to excel" at everything she did, a habit from skipping two grades in school. (This also got her into high school with Peter.) She learned all the Latin names for her plants, and was such an outstanding gardener that a hybrid Day Lily and a hybrid Rhododendron were named after her. Her love of plants was evident in her subject matter for paintings. Mary took a less competitive route, and experimented with collage and new materials, while secretly wanting to illustrate children's books. Her bright, simple figures were used for many church-related publications and mostly entertained the family.

They maintained an erudite circle of friends through many connections including Hanoverians who moved to NYC and created exciting careers –Joanie Alleman and Bill Rubin ,who founded Playbill magazine; Ann Roth, the Oscar-winning costume designer; Henry Masemer, designer for American Standard; Boris and Sophie Leavitt, who remained in Hanover and had a son the same age as myself; Justine Landis, who migrated from Manhattan with her marriage; and many, many others. Note that Ann and Henry, who had very upscale careers in NYC, both found quaint properties in Upper Bucks County, PA to escape to, and to keep a balance in their lives. They all came back to Hanover to visit families, and joked often about "What Art, here?" (Roth believes that one must leave home to find your inner artist.) Life was good. For awhile.

Peter advised us when I was thinking of going to art school. The Stella Elkins Tyler School of Art in Phila. had a good, Bohemian record, with many friends of hers, or her own instructors, who taught there – Earl Horter, Rudy Staffel, etc. It had, in the late '60's, a bucolic campus out in Elkins Park, Cheltenham – which was then still a classy neighborhood of Philadelphia. It had recently, in 1963, been taken in by Temple University as one of its campuses, after a long history as an independent art school. Tyler was

founded by the sculptor Boris Blai, an apprentice of August Rodin, in 1935 with Stella Elkins who was also a sculptor in bronze and plaster, envisioning a school that championed both the fine arts and creative thinking. They were Peter and Pearlie's contemporaries and same type of people. Or, perhaps Peter loved Tyler because they were known to bring live horses into the sculpture studio as models.

I applied, and got accepted, with Peter's encouragement, and attended with an amazing crowd of students, small campus that it was – Lee Krasner and Jackson Pollock's daughter was there, a year older than I, in 1968...I am not sure what happened, but she seems to be written out of history, as she left the school mid-year. She looked just like Lee. I can still picture her walking by the stone wall at the edge of the campus, in her vintage fur coat...a solitary, tragic soul. We had Leo, a Polish count; we had bikers on old battleship-grey Bultacos; we had a great diversity. Peter Wallach, son of Eli Wallach and Anna Jackson was a year younger than I – a happy and imaginative animated animator. Robin Reuters, of the news magnates, was a year ahead– a good person! We were a small group, in a demanding school with a high drop-out rate – 150 in the dorms, maybe 200 total, then by the end of 4 years, a graduating class of 30-50? I made it through 3 and half years, then cracked with Philadelphia summer riots and gang-wars, murders in the neighborhood and dope-drops on my apt. corner ...I left, to my parents' horror, and to disappoint all. Now I can appreciate the Surreal aspect of Peter's interest in Tyler. Peter was paying attention. I was forgiven. After all, she had done the same thing, left Philadelphia for love, quiet, and natural beauty.

She almost immediately picked up that I was back in Hanover and renovated an upper floor of her office building downtown to make an expansive NYC-style artist's loft/studio, thinking that I would live there. It was offered to me first. It was a beautiful, sophisticated space. But I was in love, and left for California. Such is the nature of a newlywed, and like Peter, I followed my heart to find my own way in the Santa Cruz Mountains. I actually returned to Tyler, to finish my degree, about 12 years later, after years of work and study in California and back in PA, Museum studies and jobs. Unconventional approaches seem to run in the family, and among friends.

"I hope you get the chance to live like you were dying."

Tim McGraw (C & W lyrics)

"Each soul must meet the morning sun, the new sweet earth and the Great Silence alone."

Oliyese, Santee Dakota physician

"What is life? It is the flash of a firefly in the night. It is the breath of a buffalo in the winter time. It is the little shadow which runs across the grass and loses itself in the sunset."

Crowfoot

I heard a horseman
Ride over the hill
The moon shone clear
The night was still.
His helm was silver
And pale was he
And the horse he rode
Was of ivory.

Walter de la Mare

"The whir of wings, as the Eagle soars, the sigh of silence as the night comes calling."

Eleanor Lois Grogan

"High in the mesa
I become
"One"
With all the dreams
I had begun."

Liz (Ruth "Jennifer" Chapin)

from Peter and Jennifer's shared journal courtesy of Christa McInturff

Somewhere in there, Peter also helped her driver and farm worker, Andy Butt, the son of her secretary, Mary. Andy had worked for the Millers, on the farm since he was 13 to 16 years of age, then was hired as an auto-mechanic in 1981. He and his wife Connie were in the process of adopting a child, when all the rules suddenly changed, requiring far more financial equity than they had. Peter offered to help, allowing them to proceed with their much-anticipated adoption. His memories of Peter are "like family." His own mother Mary grew up with Peter, her aunt Goldie Gobrecht working as live-in staff for the Myers family. Goldie "was the one who really raised Peter", according to Jim Schuman of the Hanover Historical Society. Jim lived not far away, and his own mother knew them well. Small town stuff, there, but often accurate.

Mary's memories were absolutely glowing as well. She loved Peter Miller, and often said that she could not have had a better employer. While she had started working at the mansion at the age of 14, "substituting" with her mother and aunt Anna Sheets, she was Peter's secretary from 1958 until her death. Mary described how the artistic world is "not the same as real life." And Mary thought that Peter tried to be what Hanoverians were supposed to be when she was in town, and was "maybe moreso the dutiful daughter." Mary admitted that Peter, whose name change "was motivated by the art world", was "more comfortable in one world than the other."

Andy drove Peter and "Pearlie" and often their dogs to the airport, plus frequently (at least every two weeks) back and forth between the farm and Hanover in Pennsylvania. They were usually in the Cadillac, or sometimes a big Chevy Suburban, and Peter liked to go fast, or "lickity-split." She would say "let's do it." Pearlie would only let Andy drive them, trusting him only after they spent a great deal of time together.

Andrew remembers Peter as a sweet woman who treated everyone like one big happy family, although he spent most of his time in the barns with Teddy, who also worked at Rock Raymond. Earle tried to get Andy to ride Chico, the Palomino, but Henrietta saved him just in time. It was a set-up, as Chico was a wild horse. Earle was a little wild himself. According to Andy, Earle had not been allowed to spend much time there until after his mother-in-law passed away. He had promised his prized Western 45 six-shooter and his Winchester rifle to Andy, but they never re-appeared after his death. Earle might have got along with Peter's brother, who had set up a shooting gallery in the mansion's carriage house. Andy remembers bullet holes in the ceiling from when he and Bob used to shoot there.

Chico the horse must have been quite a character. He was known to have heckled Edith and Tilano for years at the New Mexico ranch. He frequently went AWOL from the house and corral, to roam canyons and worry everyone, only to return to eat apples at Edith's back door. They loved to spoil him. Chico was eventually "retired" to the farm in Pennsylvania, where Andy Butt had his near-doom riding experience. Valocchi tells of the combined image of Earle and his horse:"I don't think that Earle was physically as big as he appeared to be but he ALWAYS looked big. Especially when he was on his horse which was, indeed and in fact, a BIG horse. My memory always refers to Earle's horse as Traveler (General Lee's horse) or "the General Lee" because Earle really looked like General Lee when he would come riding down the lane….as if he were inspecting his troops. And he always had an order to give or a complaint to air." Earle wore six guns when he rode.

All along, Peter was still painting and creating prolifically. Then, Jennifer's husband, Bob, died in Colorado, and she moved back to Hanover to care for her own aging mother. "She never let her difficulties get her down" as friend Karen remembers. Peter kept returning more regularly and spending time with her mother. Ethel Irene Hamm Myers died at the age of 102 in 1979. "Nana K", Jennifer's mother, lived into her '90s. Both daughters, friends for life, kept each other in good spirits and kept painting, kept sharing poetry and journals, all through their filial duties..

Meanwhile, the Hoffman family starts to fall apart. Trudy contracts cancer of the liver, dies within 6 months. She travels to Mexico, then Bermuda for alternative treatments. She detaches from Hanover and dies in Florida, to spare her family. Her sister, Mary also has cancer, a rare sort, and is taking the more conventional, stoic approach – surgery and chemo. She dies 6 months after Trudy. In 6 more months, Mary's son and my brother Tom, age 18, is killed in a bar fight. Then, a death every 6 months – the grandparents – Mattie Miller, then Harry Hoffman, then Irene, then Uncle Herky, followed by my father, Bob Miller. None of it is graceful, at this point. Art takes a back seat. But Jennifer is there for us, and "adopts" the younger daughters. We love her, and need the continuity.

Rock Raymond, spring house
author photo
Courtesy Linda Morrison

Then Peter has a car accident at the ranch in New Mexico in the early '80s... head injury, damage to her face followed by extensive reconstruction and recovery. Ever after, she poses for photographs slightly turned to one side. Peter must now care of her family estate, spending more time in Hanover than for many years. They decide to expand Andy Butt 's duties as a driver/mechanic. With Peter's accident and Earle getting older, they tired of driving out to New Mexico, and generally fly from Philadelphia or Baltimore airports, chartered. Hanover became Peter's office.

In a first-hand report*from 1986, the upstairs wood-paneled office, once her playroom at the mansion, still had Peter's touches–one of her own matador paintings; a Nadelman Modernist bronze, "the epitome of horse" as she said; and a small dancing woman in bronze by Earle. Many of her favorite family items remained in place – the living room was as her parents always had it, with a portrait of her father and a Steinway grand piano which Peter loves to play. The trophy room had quite an array of her father's prizes for horses, the Mallhawk Spaniel showdogs, and his barred Plymouth Rock chickens. The house was tasteful and classic, with a formal parlor featuring an aged Aubusson tapestry rug and a mantel clock from her childhood. There still is a majestic split staircase with cut glass windows on the landing, and a third-floor ballroom, along with a bowling alley in the basement. It was a home to live in and to entertain in, but became very quiet after C.N. passed away.

The Philadelphia area friends become more important, as travel becomes more difficult. Jeffrey J. Valocchi of Downingtown, remembers meeting Peter and Earle Miller in 1985, when he and his wife, Beth, moved into Harkaway Farm, the Millers' property directly adjacent to Rock Raymond Farm. "Peter's likes appeared to lean towards the more simple, less bombastic in life and art (I think Earle gave her what she needed in terms of bombastic and large living). The farmhouse was simple and the works of art they kept there were more simple and life affirming… with that touch of joy."

Jeffery Valocchi generously shares his memories. " One's first impression of Peter was that she was a strong willed, independent minded, worldly, well-read intellectual with a very pragmatic approach to life and, while she was a very refined woman and always stylish –(her jeans generally tighter than most teenagers of the day), she was more comfortable in more basic, simple surroundings." And – "One's first impression of Earle was that he was domineering, earthy, physically vibrant, and free-wheeling (leap first, think later.) One's first impression of them together was that they loved each other deeply and unequivocally."

These same years, Peter and Earle kept up their tradition of attending the Radio City Music Hall Christmas show, and invited Bill and Charlene Richards to join them at the Plaza Hotel, and the show, with dinner at the Oak Room. I can just see her delight at the big production - the multi-media dance and music extravaganza, a celebration of the Muses.

The extended Hoffman/Hollinger family picnics and celebrations continue. Jennifer is always there, and on occasion, Peter joins us for her birthdays. More Hollinger grandchildren go to art school with her blessing – Christa Bargelt (who followed the tradition of name-changing) and Carol Ann Hollinger. Both are now accomplished graphic designers.

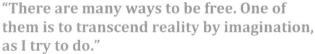
Jennifer's 82nd birthday w/Peter, Stylin' in Jennifer's studio – Jennifer and Christa, Dancers Jennifer and Heidi in J's apt.,.
All photos courtesy of Christa McInturff

"There are many ways to be free. One of them is to transcend reality by imagination, as I try to do."

Anais Nin

36

The granddaughters take Jennifer out to Peter's ranch one more time to visit, in the late '80's, just before they take their own Grand Tour of Europe, again encouraged by Peter. They treat their grandmother to stay on the Plaza in Santa Fe, at the La Fonda Hotel, where Peter and Earle often stayed when in town for events. Jennifer thought it a terrible indulgence, but loved every moment. Full circle, they were back, and visited many of the old favorite places once again.

Heidi Bargelt as icon at the ranch. Jennifer in a favorite ruin nearby. Heidi and Jennifer at the ranch. Jennifer in her element, the mountains. Peter's ranch kitchen and the living room hearth, with Earle's sculptures and painting, large *Alchemist's Tower* by Peter.   Note: Earle's sculptures on the adobe stepped mantel.
Ruth Chapin photos courtesy of Christa McInturff, except for Jennifer in the mountains. – courtesy of Karen Findling

Frank Waters, a renowned author of the Southwest, chose to write a fictional account of the life of Edith Warner and Peter Miller at this point , *The Woman at Otowi Crossing*,– it was truly one of his best venues, writing about New Mexico and the land and the people who enmeshed their lives with the Native culture and the Earth. At first, Peter was adamantly appalled, but after re-reading a few times, she saw the merit to the work. Her first reaction was quite defensive on Edith's behalf, and their privacy issues were somewhat breached. Frank answered as only a fiction writer would – that it was just a spin-off on facts, and perhaps more reality than a factual account. Peter never quite resolved that, but Jennifer felt it was OK.

There was a fire in 1986 – a wild story in itself. Joe Rishel and neighbor Jeff Valocchi both recalled this distinctly. The day before the Millers were to leave for New Mexico, they had a lunch party, attended by friends Joseph Rishel and Ann D'Harnoncourt of the Philadelphia Museum. The Miró painting, *Horse, Pipe, and Red Flower* was admired, and Peter, almost as an afterthought, suggested that, since they would be gone for months, the Museum borrow it during that time. Of course, the professional curators leaped at the chance, and Joe sent a truck over to pick it up the next morning. Millers left for New Mexico at midday, with their dogs, to make their chartered flight to the ranch.

Later that evening, Jeffrey Valocchi was alarmed to be alerted that their house on fire, and rushed over to help. He was always responsible for checking in on the place when they were gone. He tried to get inside, but was detained by the fire officials, and he agonized over their use of so much water, knowing what was in their collection. "Then I convinced the Fire Chief, when he was confident that most of the danger had passed, to let me don a fireman's coat and hat and go in. I spent the (next day) laying pages of the Blake book of poetry on the lawn, sifting pieces of Calder Mobiles from the rubble and going thru the book shelves to try and save what could be saved. The Dancer was severely burned. I was finally able to get a message to Peter and Earle in New Mexico. When they returned, Peter was pretty philosophical about things but she cried when I finally showed her the Dancer."

Joe Rishel also remembers talking with Peter and Earle the next day and he recalls that she laughed at the irony! And Jeff continues the story: "It turns out that the fire was caused by an electric short in some wires which ran under the first floor in a dirt crawl space thru which, it appeared, RAN A STREAM FROM A SPRING!!! I asked Peter about it and she was like, oh, yes there is this little stream under there in a way only Peter could express as if it was this 'dear little stream'."

Then, while they were out in New Mexico, Earle had a stroke. Peter brought him back on the usual schedule, and they lived for quite awhile in the guesthouse, as the farmhouse was being renovated. Jeffrey again tells us more: " for a man of his energy and vitality, it was quite devastating to him and at times sad and painful to watch. For those who thought he was irascible before, he was 10 times that after the stroke." Further along the process of rebuilding the original house, Peter decided to add a one-story section to make it easier for Earle to stay at home. It got complicated, as the entire house had to be emptied, with a full inventory and storage arrangements. The Philadelphia Museum of Art and Anne d'Harnoncourt were instrumental in helping, with Valocchis doing more than a neighborly duty. Peter had her hands full, but got things figured out, convoluted as they were. "She had this gentle but clear way of expressing her opinion on things without hurting anyone's feelings ."

"...she was getting ready to move Earle in (to the new addition) she said to me a few times that it was missing something and as I probed her...asking if the woodwork or some other aspect was unacceptable she would say no, that's not it....everything is fine ...it's just missing something. So one day out of the blue she calls me at my office and ask me if I could assist in getting a check for a rather large amount and could I come out to the farm and help her make sure that the purchase was ok so I get out there and there is this guy in an old station wagon and in the back is a wooden container box and I take it out and Peter tells me to be careful so I gently unscrew the panels and there in the light of day in the back of this old station wagon on a farm in little old Downingtown is what appears to be an original Braque. I look at Peter and say "you aren't serious about my being able to express any opinion about this.....as far as I know it might be an original 'Joe Schmoe the Hobo' (or something like that) and she laughs and says that of course it's original and she would know.......She hung it in the addition.....it was what was missing for Earle's new home..."

The shows did not seem to matter as much these years, but the work continued. Liz Osborne and Jimmy Leuters encouraged Peter to have a joint show of her and Earle's work at The Schoolhouse, a building on one of their farms, promoted by PAFA, with an outstanding introduction* written by Frank Goodyear III, the first professional curator at the school.

The Schoolhouse Show proved to be a celebration of Peter and Earle Miller in a timely way. Earle had died first, in 1991, age 83. Peter continued to mend and live well after the car accident, but there would be a reaction about 10 years later. Parkinson's Disease becomes part of her reality. Caregivers are recruited, plans are discussed for a conservancy for the Millers' properties.

 Just before Peter's death, Jennifer and her granddaughters, Peter's goddaughters – Christa and Heidi, and went back to celebrate connections at the ranch. They all came to tea at the ranch, and of course, danced.

It is a sad and predictable downhill from there for Jennifer, downsizing and moving into smaller apartments, then a nursing home. Peter is limited and has done the same in Downingtown, with care-

Maria Marinez' grandchildren, Heidi & Jennifer, shouting "Olé"; Facundo & Jennifer, dancing, at Peter's house.

Courtesy Christa McInturff

givers covering her needs, as they had done for Earle. Peter is holding on, makes it back to Hanover for another birthday party, bringing a vase for roses for Jennifer. The journal is passed back and forth between the friends, to share thoughts and uplifting quotes, a tradition continued until the end, even when others had to write and do things for them.

Henrietta N. Miller
HANOVER — Henrietta N. (Myers) Miller, 83, of 305 Baltimore St., died late Saturday afternoon, Oct. 19, 1996, at Rock Raymond Farms, 690 Rock Raymond Road, Downingtown.
She married the late C. Earle Miller on July 31, 1935, in Santa Fe, New Mexico. He died Jan. 14, 1991.
Born Sept. 6, 1913, in Hanover, she was the daughter of the late Clinton N. and Ethel I. (Hamm) Myers.
She graduated from Hanover Senior High School Class of 1931 and was a graduate of Arlington Hall Women's College, Washington, D.C. She was a retired artist known as Peter Miller. She was a member of several organizations who supported the Fine Arts.
She was a member of Emmanuel United Church of Christ, Hanover.
Surviving is a nephew, Dr. Robert P. Myers of Bozeman, Mont.
She was also preceded in death by her only brother, Robert C. Myers who died March 4, 1959.
The funeral service will be held at the convenience of the family.
Memorial contributions may be made to Hanover Hospital, 300 Highland Ave., Hanover, PA 17331 or Emmanuel United Church of Christ, 124 Broadway, Hanover, PA 17391.

After a long decline, Peter passed away quietly at the age of 83, on October 19. 1996. I spent the day with Jennifer, who was inconsolable. She spoke more of their "beautiful, beautiful friendship." The stories were re-told yet again...Peter's artist-stories, and friends of friends, Pueblo wisdom, and wishes that she could have given her son a mountain as a gift. All must be remembered.

There was a memorial service held at Rock Raymond Farm, for the friends and associates from the Philadelphia area. Secretary/friend Mary Butt Coleson writes for Peter, one last time. Friend Bill Richards inherits all of her paintings, because she felt that no one else wanted them or cared as much. They had often taken their framing to Tony Seraphin at the Olympia

WE CELEBRATE THE LIFE OF
HENRIETTA HYERS

"Peter"

MILLER

All of those who were fortunate to really know her and share in her life as a beautiful woman, in both body and soul, as well as a Free Spirited Artist have been truly enriched.

Her Love of Art
Was her start-
It helped her grow
Later added a glow.
The man of her life-
She became his wife.
Turtles were her charm -
As was her Rock Raymond Farm
Always a lady--
Never ever shady.
A devoted child
Even tempered & mild.
She loved to swim
and dance with HIM.
Opera, reading & dancing
Were to her truly enhancing-
To New Mexico she loved to go-
Being a tribal member added to her glow.
Generous, kind, and caring
She spent her life sharing.
We celebrate her life this day.
In a tribute that more words cannot say.

Mary Butt-Coleson

Memorial: Sunday, October 27, 1996
2:00 P.M. at her beloved
"Rock Raymond Farm"

Gallery, now the Seraphin Gallery, Phila., will be the final distributor for Peter's work, a legacy of well over 250 paintings. A show is planned for late 2015. Several venues in New Mexico are also being explored, including Santa Fe and Los Alamos.

View from Peter's ranchhouse,
Ruth Chapin photo,
Courtesy Christa McInturff, estate of Ruth K.Chapin

There was another formal service at the Emmanuel U.C.C. Church in Hanover for old friends, the town, and business associates, with Peter and Earle's names both added to the large family monument at the historic Mt. Olivet Cemetery. Peter's grand-niece Polly Powl Myers of Montana, decommissioned and sold the mansion which she inherited, while nephew Dr. Rob Myers, also of Montana, took Peter's ashes out to Santa Fe, where her heart always was. He went on one last walk up over the hills at the ranch. The land returned to the San Ildefonso Pueblo. She will always be a part of that land of enchantment, as her dear friend Peggy Pond Church first dubbed it.

 Liz Osborne has proven to be a devoted and influential friend, as well as an artist to be noted for her own work. Her relationship with Peter Miller came through PAFA, but transcended academia. They shared many ideals and a basic love of color and techniques. Elizabeth taught at PAFA for 30 years, and was instrumental in getting Peter and Earle's last show to happen. Liz and her daughter Audrey reunited with myself at Rock Raymond Farm, along with her grand-daughter, Imogene. It was an instant replay of history. The goddaughter brought her own young daughter to ride the horses and to walk at Rock Raymond Farm.

Early summer at Rock Raymond Farm
Author photo,
 courtesy of Audrey O. Cooper

The Brandywine River Museum and Conservancy was arranged as executor for the farms, worth 4.35 million dollars in 1992, in the heart of East Brandywine Township. Two-hundred and thirty acres are permanently protected by easements to the Natural Lands Trust, so that even though the Brandywine Conservancy may sell parts of the farms, they still cannot be developed further. They have sold the original Rock Raymond farm, but the fields, streams and woodlands are the same as when Peter and Earle lived there. The new owners, Linda and Jon Morrison, are dedicated horse people.

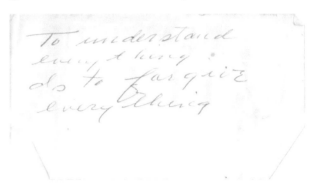

The Millers also left a large bequest to the Philadelphia Museum of Art, part of which was used

to purchase Arshile Gorky's *Woman With Palette*, painted in 1927. Gorky was an early friend of the Millers, with many overlapping connections – the Levy Gallery; his affair with Mercedes Carles, daughter of their mentor Arthur Carles; his life as neighbor of Alex Calder, Tanguy, and Masson in Connecticut, and his residence in Philadelphia. Joe Rishel curated a show of his work in 2009 at the Philadelphia Museum of Art, *"Arshile Gorky and the (Self) Invention of the Modern Artist."*

"The most powerful men are not public men. The public man is responsible and a responsible man is a slave. It is private life that governs the world."   Lord Beaconsfield

Linda Morrison & Rock Raymond Farm
Both photos by author, permission of Linda Morrison

Many critics have written that Earle Miller and Peter Miller were under-appreciated in their time, that Earle was one of the top WPA era artists, and master of lithography, while Peter had the distinction of successfully combining an ethnic symbology with her own strong modernist approach. She was a quiet, serious soul, who drew much inspiration from her farm and the ranch, as did Earle. They were truly American artists with their own styles.

The Jean and Julien Levy Foundation for the Arts will be publishing a volume of essays about all of the gallery's artists, including Peter Miller, written by Beth Gates Warren and Marie Difilippantonio in the near future. They will include extensive images of the exhibition brochures and catalogs, along with information about works included. Their working title is *Julien Levy: The Man, His Gallery; His Legacy.* Marie and I have become friends and

> "Bohemia is more than the sum of its garrets."
> R.P.Blackmur

commiserators through this process of research, and I thank her for all of our collaborative efforts, and extensive permissions! The art world is only one facet of Peter Miller's life, and of anyone's life, however dedicated we are to our various Muses. And so, there is more to the story...

Chapter Six – Women and Art and Dreams, Impossible?

While Peter Miller and Jennifer Chapin were far from feminists, they were adamantly independent souls who felt respect for everyone. They were spiritual, intellectual, and non-conforming. They quietly advocated for artists, education, and values. Honesty was important, and being true to oneself. Both of them, and all of their friends were hard-working at what they did. The old Hanover work-ethic was deeply ingrained. Yet, they found that there were conflicts between conventional lives and the demands of the Muse. "Different Yardsticks" is what Jennifer always said when someone was frustrated with acceptance issues. She was a tough cookie, full of more formal ideas about behavior and responsibilities than Peter.

The Hanover families kept up that conservative status quo as well, while so many who had moved out West found a more open vision of what was possible. The East/West dichotomy was cultural and emotional, but with glorious countryside and a venerable heritage to both. I believe that this is what motivated Peter Miller and Earle to maintain homes in both Pennsylvania and New Mexico.

It was truly impossible to tell this story without naming the overwhelming associations this era of artists and writers experienced. The contacts and readings they exchanged are part of the circular and spiraling theory of creativity. Each letter and visit was a book-list or a book swap! Cognizance and proximity can accelerate styles and production for any artist.

As well, difficulties and distractions can certainly slow things down. The Great Depression, World Wars, and politics disrupted life as everyone knew it, on whatever level of society, from the dilettantes to the drop-outs. And families! Women are particularly vulnerable to this last item. So many women artists have been lost or diminished over the years. Thank-you to writers who are reviving biographies and re-building the information base about those who hold up half the sky! Carolyn Burke, Sharon Udall, Sharon Snyder, among others, have taken time to research and inform us about these gifted women. And so, many of the most exciting and once-known-but-forgotten women artists and writers are coming out of the past, being re-discovered. Peter Miller certainly is one of these lost treasures.

Along with the handicap of information about women artists, the American cultural reticence to value the arts has taken a toll. Peter Miller and Jennifer would vouch that anyone deserves to

42

"the poet is an anomaly in our culture. Goal of culture=money & power. NOT exactly what poetry is about...anything the human mind and unconscious can produce. INFINITE."

Stanley Kunitz

"He paints as other men must dream..and his visions take him back thousands of years of world sub-consciousness. He belongs to no one medium, but to all."

Henry Miller: about Rogaway, NM painter

Grandmother Earth is alive
The mountains have souls
The Trees sing late at night
Grains of sand can speak.
It's just that no one listens.

W.Micheal Gear and Kathleen O'Neal Gear, *People of the Nightland*

"Rocks have existed since the beginning of the Earth. They have seen and heard everyting. They speak almost as slowly as they move. They teach you about patience, reliability, and age-old wisdom."

Rick Bass, *the Lives of Rocks*

"...writing for me is a way of understanding what is happening to me, of thinking hard things out...for art is order, but it is made out of the chaos of life...I am fully myself perhaps only when I am creating."

May Sarton, *At Seventy, a journal*

be valued as an artist. They and their peers made a point to compete and to educate their younger generation to be committed to the higher principles of Art, as formal quality and craft are the final measures. And they all evolved through an exciting and demanding time of changes in the field.

Fairfield Porter, in the '50s, wrote of the venerable Pennsylvania Academy artist Eakins, calling him a "self-righteous Philadelphian" who had to convince himself that art (painting) was work. There was such a struggle to let go of that work ethic and just enjoy the process. So, the later generations of painters had learned to trust their eyes, and deal with the conflicts of "the decorum of social structure" versus the "wild permissiveness of inner life" as Stanley Kunitz described it.

Along with a general cultural avoidance of art is the big issue of spirituality and dreams! The Native Americans do not discern as much between the worlds of dream and reality. Peter Miller and her "spiritual guide" Edith Warner, and also Jennifer Chapin corresponded about revelations and the language of dreams and ancient artifacts. Everything is alive, has a spirit. And the Buddhists, along with many Eastern religions acknowledge this as well. Perhaps the New Physics will clarify this beyond doubt. Stephen Hawking writes that "To come to one of my lectures would be the same as attending a Buddhist lecture. We are saying the same thing." Metaphysics and Magic and the Earth! People shy away from the New Age label on thoughts, it being "whooo-whoo" or over-exploited these years. But the basis is important, perhaps to survival.

Robert J. Goldwater (1907-1973), who was married to Louise Bourgeois (a French student of Ferdinand Leger) and a friend of Peter's, wrote about this pertaining to her artwork, in the catalog for her premier show at Julien Levy's gallery. Like Levy, he was one of the first grads of Harvard to study Modern Art. He was a professor of art at the time, but Goldwater went on to become a critic, scholar, and expert on primitive art for the Rockefeller's Museum of Primitive Art, NYC. In the Levy Archives he explains a bit about symbols and perspective:

"For five hundred years painting has been called a window, and through that window we have looked at space – space represented (by perspective), or space suggested (by the relations of forms). Though painters have cut that space at the

43

edges… or more recently, exaggerated it,… its idea obsesses them still.

"All life is better understood as community rather than commodity."
Aldo Leopold

The Indians, fortunately, painted on the ground. For this reason – and for many others – their painting had no visible relation to the world through which we walk. Each painting was at once everywhere and nowhere, was, as we say, a symbol. Spatially it was absolute: expansion without direction, forms that were weightless …because they had never been considered in relation to gravity. There was no representation of reality, but during its brief existence each picture gathered the forces of reality into itself, became powerful, potentially dangerous, and had to be destroyed.

To point out that Peter Miller has absorbed some of the shapes of Miró - who gave those shapes their power in a heightening of space; and that she has employed a number of the symbols of Indian sand and rock painting is only to make obvious the fact that every painter comes from somewhere. But more and more she has merged the two, has taken the sophisticated shapes and given them a primitive setting, put them in an atmosphere of earthen colors, coppers, greys, and browns, where they exist oblivious of a world of gravity and the upright spectator. Washing her paint down to its thinnest she has created, filled, suffused, and varied atmosphere that has something to of the distant and absolute qualities of the Indian paintings…" He liked that her paintings "bring before us brilliant, symbolic creatures who move fluidly through an unending continuum."

Sharing dreams, or a collective subconscious, is more normal to a Pueblo community, used to living with rhythms of nature and a sense of wholeness. Edith Warner often wrote to Peter about "revelations" in her perceptions of community and creativity. Creativity is more a state of mind, heart, and soul, no matter how many people are around, however the balance and the reserves must be kept and honored. Form and symbol can be links to nature, as Peter used. Many others began just before her, with the traditions of myth and magic. Others who included these archetypes in their work include Kahlo, O'Keefe, and Carr, all women painters who were both modern and ancient in their consciousness.

Interestingly, both Emily Carr and Georgia O'Keefe

Declaration of the Independence of the Imagination and Rights of Man to His Own Madness (excerpts)

"…in confirmation of the above, we announce these truths: that all men are equal in their madness, and that madness (visceral cosmos of the subconscious) constitutes the common base of the human spirit…

The rights of man to his own madness are constantly threatened, and treated in a manner that one may without exaggeration call 'provincial' by false 'practical-rational' hierarchies. The history of the true creative artist is filled with the buses and encroachments by means of which an absolute tyranny is imposed by the industrial mind over the new creative ideas of the poetic mind…."
Salvador Dali, 1938

44

kept libraries of books filled with writings of D.H.Lawrence, Freud, Jung, and Neitzche. All studied archetypes and nature, and relationships. Frieda Kahlo had shown at the Levy Gallery, and they all knew Steiglitz, of course. The awareness of indigenous peoples was growing.

In Levy's note about "this continent of Dream has always been available to mankind," he jokes about Chirico being a stowaway on the expedition to explore this subconscious continent. But he applauds Dali for his convictions and was a bit player in the dropping of 100's of Dali's manifestos from an airplane in 1938, after his concepts were censored for the World's Fair. Levy writes: "Between the notion that a lucid intelligence such as Salvador Dali's should be considered insane, and the oppressive feeling that the helpless, fumbling gestures of the financial and political leaders of our realistic society are to be judged competent and trustworthy, there seemed a gap in reasoning."
Ha, some things never change!

> "A myth is a public dream; a dream is a private myth."
> Joseph Campbell

Dr. Fred Alan Wolf a quantum physicist and metaphysicist, combines many ideas that fascinated Peter Miller and her friends. He writes that the law of attraction is "not wishful thinking or imaginary craziness – I'm talking from a deeper, basic understanding. Quantum physics really begins to point to this discovery…you can't have a Universe without mind entering into it and that the mind is actually shaping the very thing that is being perceived." Native Americans have known this all along. While the Western world is not comfortable with challenges to "control or proof" world view, it seems that this is truly the last frontier for humans. As Einstein said "Imagination is everything. It is the preview of life's coming attractions."

"The worth of art could also lie in the happiness it brought its creator, no?"

Varita Sankaran, *Watermark*

"A truly creative person rids him or herself of all self-imposed limitations."

Gerald G. Jampolsky, MD & Diane V. Circh-Crone

"The body is a cage, so is the mind."

Unknown

"Art is like love, you have to be willing to make a fool of yourself."

Leah Stewart, *Husband and Wife*

"Nature never stays still"

Monet

"What a man thinks of himself, that it is which determines, or rather, it dictates his fate."

Thoreau

"I hope you love birds, too. It is economical. It saves going to heaven."

"My friends are my estate."   Emily Dickinson

"Wherever you look, nothing sanctifies new money more quickly than the smell of horse manure."   Michael Korda
(one for Earle!)

"An act of pure attention, if you are capable of it, will bring its own answer."   D. H Lawrence

To pay attention to our dreams and accept our links to the collective subconscious is to open our imaginations. Peter Miller, Jennifer Chapin, and Trudi Hollinger were all open and active, yet solitude and nature combined to make their art, to enable them to find themselves, and to connect to a rich inner world. Peter often spoke of having a teacher appear when needed.

For Peter and Jennifer, the inner experience and their relationship with nature triggered primordial, archetypal images. Peter wrote of images "older than memory." Trudi learned to be expressive, to trust more than her eye. "You can't depend on your eyes when you imagination is out of focus." (Mark Twain)

The Navaho and Hopi/Mayan (Pueblo) peoples had some differences in their art – the first more portable and the second more ritual, but all utilized symbols and the sensibilities of individuals within a community. It can be done, whether we are introverts or extroverts. Sometimes this requires a little help from our friends.

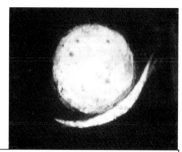

One of Peter's paintings which hangs in her old home, now owned and maintained by the Hanover Historical Society, Looks like a pictograph that was seen above a large spring, on rock bluffs over the Missouri River. It is ancient, and similar ones are found all around the world. It possibly represents a supernova that appeared in Ad. 1054. as written by William Least-Heat Moon. Physics, again?
Or some impossible past-life?

Untitled Peter Miller oil
Photo by the author
Courtesy of the Hanover Area
Historical Society

Chapter Seven – Full Circle

An unknown person wrote that "A friend is someone who knows the song in your heart and can sing it back to you when you have forgotten the words." Peter and Jennifer did this for each other. May we all have such friends, and may I suggest that our communities need this, as well.

The forward discoveries from researching and writing this kind of collage-book, with so many references and general chaos-theory information, are ones of a positive nature. I think of seeds planted, roots and trees, and arboretums, and wild vibrant growth of personalities and art, and the deep loam of a collective imagination. Tilano's message that laughter is of the gods is with us, too.

Circular thinking and networks of women may yet save the world. There is a group that I don't think Peter and Jennifer or my elders knew of, but they would absolutely love it - The Thirteen Indigenous Grandmothers Council who work to heal and to make peace among all people. If freeing ourselves to trust, and to create, will get us into the next evolution, perhaps the Aquarian Age, after all, I am all for it.

At the end of her life, Peter Miller requested time with a guru, arranged by Charlene Richards. We are told that Peter's totem is the turtle. This figure appears in many of her paintings. It is written that the tortoise symbolizes longevity, simplicity, and slowing down long enough to really pay attention.

Samuel Hazo, the first state poet of Pennsylvania, in *A Flight to Elsewhere* wrote *"Tortoise Time":*

...At peace in place
He comes from where he was
To where he'll be like afterthought's
caboose.
...if home is what he is, he's home
to start with since he moves
to go away.
           Aesop understood.

Peter made it back to her beloved New Mexico and someday Jennifer will make it back to her Wild Horse Mesa. Full circle. The generations continue, whether blood-related or spirit-sisters or godchildren. The circle only widens.

Found objects, Jennifer, Peter, and many more. Author photo

Gallery

works by Peter Miller

Untitled, early sketches, Peter Miller

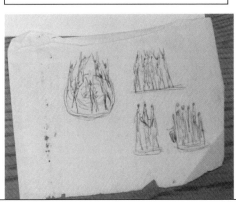

These early works were found under the floor, in the PA farmhouse.

Photography by Andrea Miller Theisson   Courtesy of the Brandywine River Museum of Art

Right & below: ***Marigold***
Signed on back, as usual, author photo
Courtesy Hanover Area Historical Society

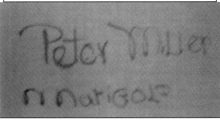

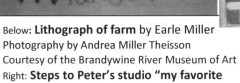

Below: **Lithograph of farm** by Earle Miller
Photography by Andrea Miller Theisson
Courtesy of the Brandywine River Museum of Art
Right: **Steps to Peter's studio "my favorite walk in the world"**
Photo by author   Courtesy of Linda Morrison

48

Interior of Peter Miller studio, Rock Raymond Farm   courtesy of Bill Richards

Below: **Large Tortoise** by Peter Miller
        Courtesy of Bill Richards
    Cat and Mesa by Peter Miller
Author photo, Courtesy of Hanover Area Historical Society
Right: **Desert Cat** by Peter Miller
        Courtesy of Christa McInturff

Right-
Peter's
Work
from
ranch

Photo by
Ruth
Chapin
Courtesy
Chirsta
McInturff

Above: ***King and Queen*** by Peter Miller
Courtesy of Christa McInturff

Below: ***The Boss*** by Peter Miller
Courtesy of Christa McInturff

The Bird Priest by Peter Miller
Courtesy of private collector

Title Unknown, work from Ranchhouse
Photo by Ruth Chapin   Courtesy of Christa McInturff

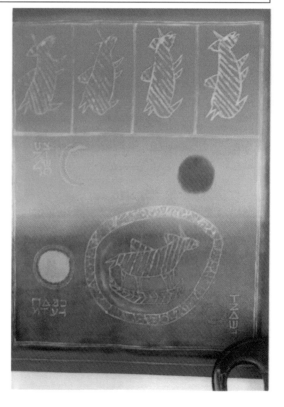

50

Right: Untitled sketch, author believes may be of friend Peggy Pond Church, declared a Santa Fe Living Treasure in 1986, and done later when Peter's hands were shaky with Parkinson's.
Photography by Andrea Miller Theisson
Courtesy of the Brandywine River Museum of Art

Left: *Snail with Umbrella*

Below: *Snake Loop*

Courtesy of Bill Richards

Left: *Chrysallis*

Courtesy of Bill Richards

Below: Peter's studio in New Mexico

Courtesy of Christa McInturff, estate of Ruth Chapin

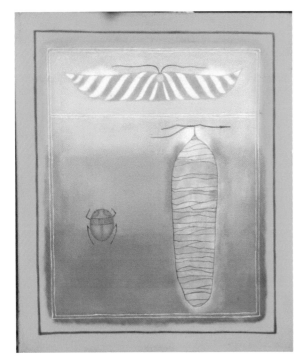

51

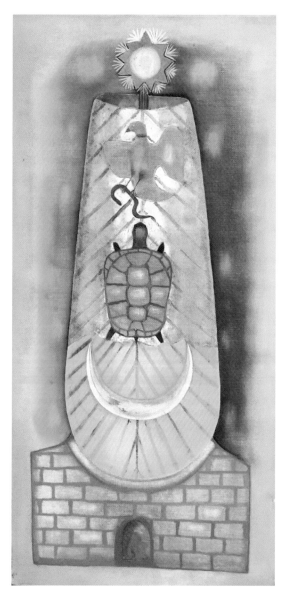

The Alchemist's Tower

Photo by author   Courtesy of Hanover Area Historical Society

Left: **Turtle Totem**

Bottom Left: show postcard, **Dance Paddles**

Below: **painted stones** by Peter Miller

Notes: All of Peter Miller's paintings are oils.

Her totem was the turtle.

All of these paintings are fairly large. See her studio photos to compare scale of canvases. These have been in storage for some time, the sizes are unavailable at publication.

The painted stones are in a damaged photo, possibly from the fire at Rock Raymond.
These three images, left and below, Courtesy of Bill Richards

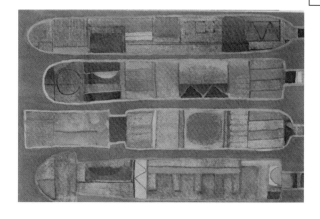

52

works by C. Earle Miller

Untitled dancer and *Rock Sound, Eleuthera* (Bahamas)
Photography by Andrea Miller Theisson   Courtesy of the Brandywine River Museum of Art

Above: Untitled Mediterranean lithograph

Above: Untitled lithograph   2 photos by author
Courtesy of Hanover Area Historical Society

Above: Untitled sketch for a sculpture by Earle
Photography by Andrea Miller Theisson
Courtesy of the Brandywine River Museum of Art

Right: Horse and Trees lithograph
Photo Courtesy of Christa McInturff, estate of Ruth Chapin

53

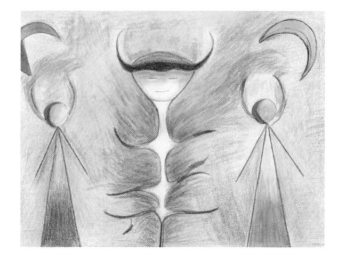

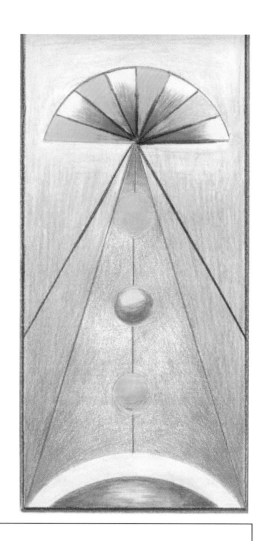

works by Jennifer Chapin

Untitled, colored pencil and mixed media, stone and leather doll   courtesy of Christa McInturff
Notes; Ruth Chapin "Jennifer" had a twin brother who died as an infant, many images relate to this.

Untitled geometric and rock forms, colored pencil and ink

Courtesy of Christa McInturff, Estate of Ruth Kump Chapin

Untitled oil painting, and oil image with scriffito on clay, "Jennifer's corner" at author's home with her rocks and a small scriffito pot by Hilda Whitegoat, Navaho.

Photo by the author

works by
Trudi Hoffman Hollinger

early work

Note that Trudi's early work was very austere and somewhat repressed. She became known for her later work, vibrant and loose palette-knife paintings and relaxed, simplified watercolors. Unfortunately, the watercolors are all under glass and difficult to photograph, and many paintings are unavailable for photography. The large garden and plant paintings are outstanding.

later work -

right: *Out of the Darkness,*
oil and lacquer

below: Untitled beach scene, watercolor

Photography by author

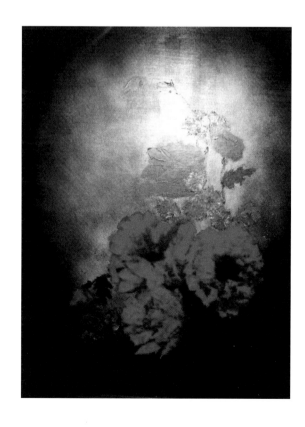

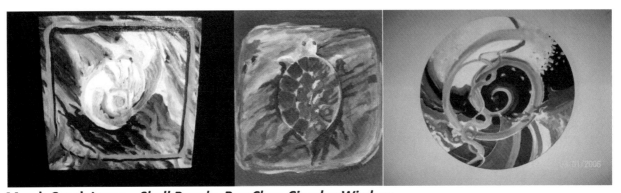

Marsh Creek Icons – *Shell People, Box Clan; Circular Wisdom*
Taos Magic (below); *Walking Pojoaque*(rt), **Druid Clan Totem** (below)

> **work by Andrea Miller Theisson**
> daughter of Mary Hoffman Miller, friend of Jennifer
> paintweaver

Coriolis, (below); *Creek Lights* (right)

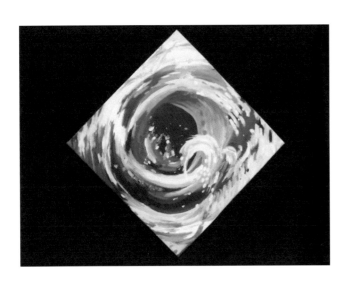

work by Christa Bargelt McInturff
charcoal work, late 1980's, now graphic designer
Granddaughter of "Jennifer" Ruth Chapin and Trudi Hoffman Hollinger,
goddaughter of Peter Miller

work by Carol Hollinger.
Graphic designer.
Granddaughter of Trudi Hoffman Hollinger

Exhibitions and Reviews

Markings, 1992 retrospective   Reprinted with permission, Frank Goodyear Jr.

"Art and Artmaking have always been an integral part of Peter and Earle Miller's lives. They consistently challenged themselves to express, through art, their own personal feelings and convictions. That legacy, their art work, is an important window in their souls."

About Peter and Earle Miller

"There is a fullness and joy that defines Peter Miller. The same 'bigness in heart and mind,' that she wrote in reminiscing about her father, can be written about her. That 'bigness' also defines her art.

Peter Miller has never ceased to wrap her arms around the fullness of life, born of a lifelong affair with nature. She loves the flowers that grow wild in the fields of her native Pennsylvania, the deep blue sky of New Mexico, the swooping birds, and radiant butterflies; she calls the trees her 'brother and sisters.' Peter sees magic, mystery, and romance in nature; it feeds her imagination and excites her fantasies. She marvels at nature's order; its rhythms, its logic, its sensibility. She is its perennial student. Hand her a fieldstone, she holds it caressingly in her hands, rubbing it repeatedly to enjoy its surface. She finds beauty wherever beauty resides, often in the smallest and most unassuming of things.

Earle shared in Peter's love of nature. A robust and hearty man, he too was inspired by nature's magnitude and awed by nature's power. He was never more content than when, astride his favorite horse, he found himself amid nature's wonders.

Peter Miller is also that rare combination of incurable romantic and classical empiricist. Hers is a constant search for knowledge about the order of the universe. Nowhere is that search more rigorous than in her studio. Situated in an adjacent outbuilding, she has made the same short walk to the studio literally thousands of times – ascending from below, up three steps, then five more, and then the final two before the prospect of entry. She calls it "her favorite walk in the world." Bathed on a bright day in the radiance of a clear northern light, the studio is a small, private sanctuary, built into the side of a steep grassy hill. It expresses worlds about its owner.

The first impression of the studio is of all these joyful paintings crowding in, eager for attention, each with its own story to tell, and of the implements of their making, paintbrushes and now stiff wipe-off rags used to create thin veils of stained color on the canvas surface. One moves about the tight space with caution and expectation. There is so much to knock against, and much from which to learn. A closer look reveals that knowledge. A handwritten pencil notation on the wall speaks to the peripatetic and inexplicable forces of inspiration; the challenge of making art, and the divine protection afforded its makers for their courage. It is George Santayana's implied blessing on this studio of art. Close by, a similar wall notation, a line from

Robert Frost, invokes the phenomena of natural wonders, words seemingly written for Peter. Postcards of an archaic Greek *kouros* and an Egyptian diety, notebooks of photographs of famous Italian Renaissance monuments visited with her husband, and reproductions of works by Rembrandt and Durer, lost in a drawer among the artists own drawings, imply her admiration. Through all of this, one feels the presence of a cultivated mind and an eye sensitive to form.

If the words of poets and the images of art help to reveal the artist's mind, then so, too, does the other dominant studio presence, found objects from nature: baskets of seashells, accumulations of weathered stones, patterned turtles' shells, bird feathers, and oddly configured pieces of wood. One can imagine the joy of discovery of these simple but beautiful natural objects, found over the years on the countless tramps through woods and fields, or brought to her by young children who knew where to take their own discoveries.

About their Art

As a child Peter Miller proclaimed that she would be a poet and a dancer. These she has been, but more than anything, with her husband Earle, a graduate of the Pennsylvania Academy of Fine Arts, she has been an artist all of her life. What defines Peter's art? What defines Earle's art?

A passionate and sensual woman, Peter has a native sense of the underlying natural order of the universe. Reverential of that order but equally fascinated by its inexplicability, she plumbs the mysteries of the universe, of creation and regeneration, as her own personal challenges. So too is Peter's art both reasoned and intuitive, passionate and restrained. She expresses joy in color, celebrated in rich, lush surfaces. Color in Peter Miller's work can also be subtle, tonal, even recessive, expressive of her quieter, more reflective moods. There is a singular force of design in the work, with large, bold, outlined forms, symbolist in intent; and there is a quasi-minimalist use of form; ordered, progressive, and empirical. And there is her use of multiple reference: the Cubism of Picasso and Braque; the fantasies of Miró; the whimsies of Klee; the color of her teacher Carles; the magic Realism of American painting of the 1940's; the geometry of Amish quilts and American hooked rugs; signs and symbols of her beloved Native Americans; primitive pictographs made by anonymous artists in New Mexico. Remarkably, the assimilation of these references finds a personal resolution in her work that may be best characterized as 'the Peter Miller ordering of the world.'

Earle Miller's work, unlike Peter's, grew out of a design background, and subsequently, the influence of his teacher Earle Horter, at the Pennsylvania Academy, where he was also exposed to printmaking and figurative traditions. Earle Miller's prints, woodcuts andlithographs reveal some of the stylization of the 1930s and 1940s. As Peter Miller often celebrated color, Earle's prints, especially a series of lithographs on bullfighting, celebrated the power and the richness of the color black. Like his wife, his works also reveal a passion for strong contours and forceful design. Earle employs the element of motion in his work, whereas Peter's forms are static, like specimens in a display case.

Earle's love of contour, motion, and limited coloration served him well when he turned to making sculpture. He could portray the speed of a galloping horse, the power of a charging bull, or the sensuous grace of a dancing figure with equal conviction. Abstracted, one feels the influence of Eli Nadelman's work in alone, solitary figure. Earl Miller's sculpture also expressed the sensibility of its maker to his materials.

Earle and Peter Miller created their own 'ordering of the world.' Their art is independent. It tells its own story, but also speaks to shared feelings and convictions, aesthetic and otherwise. It is a marriage of equals."

Frank H. Goodyear, Jr.
July 31, 1992
Pennsylvania Academy of the Fine Arts

Peter Miller- exhibitions

SELECTED ONE-PERSON SHOWS

Metaphysical Paintings, the Grand Gallery, Wilmington, DE

Metaphysical Paintings, Larcada Gallery, New York, NY

Santa Fe Museum, Santa Fe, NM

Julien Levy Gallery (two shows), New York, NY (May 1944, Oct.1945)

Museum of Fine Arts, Houston, TX

California Palace of Fine Arts, San Francisco, CA (fall, 1946)

Alfred Rogaway Gallery, Albuquerque, NM (1960, 1961)

Guadalupe Gallery, Albuquerque, NM

Dallas Museum of Art, Dallas, TX

Vincent Garofilo Gallery, Albuquerque, NM

Cosmopolitan Club, Philadelphia, PA

Peale Club of the Pennsylvania Academy of the Fine Arts, Philadelphia, PA

Penn Art Center, Philadelphia, PA

SELECTED GROUP EXHIBITIONS

C.Earle Miller and Peter Miller, Downingtown, PA

C. Earle Miller and Peter Miller, Pennsylvania Academy of the Fine Arts, Philadelphia, PA

Philadelphia Museum of Art, Philadelphia, PA

Philadelphia Art Alliance, Philadelphia, PA

Moore College of Art, Philadelphia, PA

Art of This Century – The Women , Julien Levy Gallery, New York, NY

Philadelphia Academy of the Fine Arts Annuals, Philadelphia, PA

This list is from the brochure of the Levy Gallery exhibition, *Art of This Century-The Women,* circa early 1940's.

Courtesy of Bill Richards

Note: # 10, Leonore Krassner later changed her name to Lee Krasner, who married Jackson Pollock, and yes, that really is THE Gypsy Rose Lee, who did some painting and was considered a Surrealist!

PAINTINGS & SCULPTURE
by

1. VIRGINIA ADMIRAL	16. PETER MILLER
2. NELL BLAINE	17. ANNE NEAGOE
3. LOUISE BOURGEOIS	18. ALICE PAALEN
4. ZENIA CAGE	19. IRENE RICE PEREIRA
5. LEONORA CARRINGTON	20. HELEN PHILLIPS
6. RONNIE ELLIOT	21. BARBARA REIS
7. PEARL FINE	22. KAY SAGE
8. ANNIE HARVEY	23. SONIA SEKULA
9. FANNIE HILLSMITH	24. JANET SOBEL
10. LEONORE KRASSNER	25. HEDDA STERNE
11. JACQUELINE LAMBA	26. JULIA THECLA
12. GYPSY ROSE LEE	27. PEGEEN VAIL
13. MURIEL LEVY	28. ISABELLE WALDBERG
14. LOREN MacIVER	29. CHARMION WIEGAND
15. McKEE	30. CATHERINE YARROW

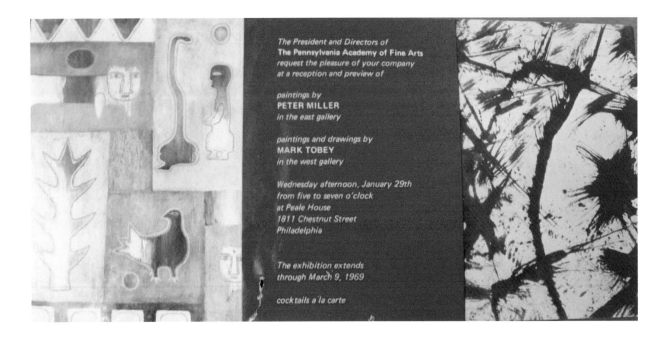

P.A.F.A. flyer courtesy of Bill Richards

(more from Peter and Jennifer's journal:)

"I will seek the place where gypsies roam and strange, wild songs are sung; I will find once more the magic paths I knew when the world was young, And the stars will give me comradeship and the wind will be my friend, And I will send you the gold that lies at the rainbow's end. "

from *The Vagrant* by Pauline Slender

"I am almost always religious on a sunny day." Byron

"My spirit eyes see the colors and textures and shapes moving up through
My spirit entering the brush and making my tracks on the canvas and the paper. "

"Liz" Ruth "Jennifer" Chapin

Select Bibliography, Interviews and Websites

Articles-
Abatemarco, Michael. For the New Mexican column: "New Mexico's Old Masters; Jaune Quick-to-See vs. the Petroglyph Killers." *The New Mexican* ; January 27-February 2, 2012.

Books-
Bachrach, Arthur J. *D.H.Lawrence in New Mexico; "The Time is Different There."* Albuquerque, NM: University of New Mexico Press, 2006.

Bandelier, Adolph Francis Alphonse. *The Delight Makers.* Lexington, KY: Forgotten Books, (first publilshed 1890) republished 2008. www.forgottenbooks.org

Brown, Rita Mae. *Starting From Scratch; A Different Kind of Writer's Manual.* Toronto/NY: Bantam Books, 2008.

Burke, Carolyn. *Becoming Modern: the Life of Mina Loy;* New York, NY: Farrar, Straus and Giroux, 1996.

Burke, Carolyn. *Lee Miller: A Life;* Chicago,IL; University of Chicago Press, 2007.

Burns, Patrick, ed. *In the Shadow of Los Alamos; Selected Writings of Edith Warner.* Albuquerque, NM: University of New Mexico Press, 2001.

Church, Peggy Pond. *This Dancing Ground of Sky –the selected poetry*; Santa Fe, NM: Red Crane Books, 1993.

Church, Peggy Pond. *The House at Otowi Bridge; The Story of Edith Warner and Los Alamos.* Albuquerque, NM: University of New Mexico Press, 1959, 1960, 4th printing 1973.

Conant, Jennet. *109 East Palace; Robert Oppenheimer and the Secret City of Los Alamos.* New York,NY: Simon & Schuster, 2005.

Cozzalino, Robert. *Elizabeth Osborne- The Color of Light*; Piermont, NH: Pennsylvania Academy of Art and Bunker Hill Publishing, 2009.

Eldredge, Charles C.; Schimmel, Julie; Truetter, William H. *Art in New Mexico, 1900-1945 Paths to Taos and Santa Fe;* New York, NY: National Museum of American Art Smithsonian Institution/ Abbeville Press, 1986.

Giroud, Vincent. *"Picasso and Gertrude Stein"*. *The Metropolitan Museum of Art Bulletin*, reprint. New Haven, CT: Yale University Press, 2006.

Hignett, Sean. *Brett: From Bloomsbury to New Mexico, a Biography*; New York: Franklin Watts, 1984.

64

Jenkinson, Clay S. *A Free and Hardy Life – Theodore Roosevelt's Sojourn in the American West.* Washburn, ND: Dakota Institute Press, 2011

Levy, Julien. *Memoir of an Art Gallery;* New York, NY; G.P. Putnam's Sons, 1977

Perl, Jed. *New Art City – Manhattan at Mid-Century;* New York, NY: Vintage Books, 2005.

Ray, Charles H. PhD.; Anderson, Sherry Ruth PhD. *The Cultural Creatives – How 50 Million People Are Changing the World;* New York, New York: Harmony/Random House, Inc., 2000.

Reichard, Gladys A. *Navaho Religion; A Study of Symbolism;* Princeton, NJ: Princeton University Press, 1950, 1977.

Snyder, Sharon. *At Home on the Slopes of Mountains – the Story of Peggy Pond Church;* Los Alamos,NM:Los Alamos Historical Society Publications, 2011.

Udall, Sharon Rohlfsen. *Carr, O'Keefe, Kahlo - Places of their Own*; China: Yale University, 2000.

Waters, Frank. *The Woman at Otowi Crossing; a novel.* Athens, OH: Swallow Press/ Ohio University Press, 1966, revised 1987.

Wickenden, Dorothy. *Nothing Daunted; The Unexpected Education of Two Society Girls in the West.* New York: Scribner, 2011.

Oral Histories, Interviews, Unpublished Memoirs, Misc.-
Butt-Coleson, Mary Gobrecht
Butt, Andrew
Chapin, Ruth Kump Bargelt.
DiFilippantonio, Marie. Archivist for Jean & Julien Levy Foundation, NYC
Findling, Karen.
Geiselman, Jane.
Goodyear, Frank
Hollinger, Carol.
McBride, Heidi Bargelt.
McInturff, Christa Bargelt.
Osborne, Elizabeth
Pfaff, Clifford
Richards, Bill and Charlene
Rishel, Joseph (Philadelphia Museum of Art)
Rost, Lizbeth Hollinger Bargelt Maclane.
Roth, Ann
Schuman, Jim (Hanover Area Historical Society)
Shutt, Irene
Stanislaw, Gail. (Librarian, Brandywine River Museum, Chadds Ford, PA)

Websites –Resources

Andrea Miller Theisson http://www.paintweaver.com/
http://www.andreamillertheisson.blogspot.com/
Bill Richards http://billrichardsstudio.com
http://northeastcenter.com/profile-richards.htm
Hanover Area Historical Society http://www.hahs.us/
Liz Osborne
http://www.gorkysgranddaughter.com/2012/09/elizabeth-osborne-august-2012.html

Thirteen Indigenous Grandmothers Council http://www.grandmotherscouncil.org/

Notes (all book references* are in bibliography)

Chapter One –

*unless otherwise noted, all photos in this chapter are from Ruth Kump Chapin, courtesy of Christa McInturff.

*A History of the Tewa by Andrea M. Theisson , copyright 2010
The Tewa, a linguistic group of Pueblo Native American peoples, date much further back into time than recorded history. Northern New Mexico still has five groups who speak derivatives of the Tewa language, on or near the Rio Grande, north of Santa Fe. The communities are Nambe, Pojoaque, San Ildefonso, San Juan, Santa Clara and Tesuque. There is also a Hano group, established in eastern Arizona after 1694, a result of the rebellion of 1680-92, although they were almost decimated by smallpox in the early 1900's.
Traditional archaeology has the original tribes of the Tewa descended from groups of hunters and gatherers who came to the region over 10,000 years ago, probably migrating from Central America, and Mexico. The People themselves say that they have always been here. More recently, the Pueblo people or Anasazi (pre-Spanish)came from Chaco Canyon and Mesa Verde , or the Four Corners area, around 1200 to 1500 AD to occupy the mesas and cliffs of the Pajarito Plateau, mostly present-day Bandelier National Monument. Many present-day Pueblo people prefer to call this original community the "Ancestral Pueblo People."
The Bandelier region supported farmers who grew maize, or corn, beans and squash, and also the harvest of deer, rabbits, other small game and birds. Cotton was cultivated and woven into garments. Yucca-fiber was used along with feathers in winter garments, and tools were developed as well as traded with Southern peoples of Mexico and Baja.
By the mid-1200's, the villages were at their peak. Drought and other factors created the migrations to the present pueblos - Nambe, which translates as "Mound of Earth in the Corner," Pojoaque or "Water Drinking Place," San Ildefonso or "Where the Water Cuts Through," Ohkay Owingeh or San Juan which means "Village of the Strong People," Santa Clara or "Valley of the Wild Roses," and Tesuque or "Cottonwood Tree Place."
The sacred sites, ancestral stories and petroglyphs, coiled hair and costumes, and the Creation myths of the Tewa are all inter-related to a common history, with some Mayan motifs recurring. Traditions of fine pottery were revived in the 20th Century, noting efforts by Maria Martinez and family with their black-ware. And, along with embroidery, weaving, and jewelry, these skills are being taught and exhibited at the new Poeh Museum and Cultural Center in Pojoaque. This unique center has all six-Tewa-speaking tribes represented and provides a venue for teaching, exhibiting and interpreting their art, word and history, archiving photographs as well as providing contemporary studios and workshops.
Festivals, Dances and Feast Days are all celebrated traditionally. Many are open to the public, but each Pueblo is different. The dates reflect the generations of exposure to the Spanish culture, and are often combined with Catholic holidays along with the original Native celebrations.

Many of the Pueblos are now hosting Gaming establishments such as the huge and spectacular Buffalo Thunder Resort . clubs, services, Broadband Internet, wellness centers and colleges for their people. A written language has been developed and the verbal language is being taught with a passion. Their culture will survive!
*see Bibliography; Burns, Patrick.

Chapter Two –

*Sherman's Farm was described by Andy Butt, and he claims there is an old slave graveyard on the property, and secret stairways to hiding compartments from Underground Railroad days.

*Hanover Public Library History – In 1875, Dr. J. P. Smith and his wife, Gabriella bequeathed $42,036.10 for a Town Hall, of which a part is to be a public reading room. Then in 1879, George Metzer donated $1,900. To be invested in an endowment for a Civic League, to become the Library Association. Then, Mr. & Mrs. H.E. Young donated a grand building to honor their son, Edward Etzler Young, who died early in life. The Yond Memorial Library opened on Oct. 3, 1911. Mabel Champlin Wolcott was the first librarian. She was still there when the author started using the library in the early 1950's. The founders are a branch of Rita Mae Brown's mother's family. When the author worked there in the 1970's, we purchased all of Brown's available books! And, we then started a series of fine art shows.

*The Hanover ShoeFarms - http://www.hanoverpa.com/

"In the early 1900's Lawrence B. Sheppard, then in his twenties and a junior partner in the Hanover Shoe Company, supplied the drive and vision to transform the Hanover Shoe Stables into Hanover Shoe Farms. (author's note: C.N. Myers was part-owner of the farms, but also had several other interests – Blue Bar Kennels showdogs, and prize-winning Barred Plymouth Rock poultry. The Horse farms were a joint effort, but L.B. Sheppard was most active.)This transformation began in 1922 when Sheppard began replacing the modest, mediocre stock with some of the finest racehorse of the era, with Baron Worthy and Peter Manning among them. But it was in 1926, when Lawrence Sheppard boldly bought a 69-horse package from the estate of A.B. Coxe, that Hanover truly burst upon the national scene.

For the next 42 years, young Sheppard was determined to keep Hanover as "The greatest name in harness racing." He got no argument from the woman he married, a San Antonio belle named Charlotte Cassin Newton, who shared his great love of horses. And his constant quest for excellence caused him to select John F. Simpson, a successful young horseman, as his ultimate successor at the helm of Hanover Shoe Farms. The history of any breeding farm is a chronicle of its stallions. Hanover has historically been home to many of the sport's most prolific sires. From the early years of harness racing's first Hambletonian winner Guy McKinney and the world champions Dean Hanover and Billy Direct; to the post World War II era of Star's Pride, Adios and Tar Heel; to the late 70s, 80s and early 90s with Super Bowl and Albatross.

In 2001, Hanover Shoe Farms-bred colts and fillies set the all-time earnings record regardless of breed with a total of $21,372,418."

P.O. Box 339 Route 194 South
Hanover, PA 17331
Phone: 717-637-8931
Fax: 717-637-6766
The farm is open to visits by the public, 7 days a week during daylight hours. All tours are self-guided. If you come between the hours of 8:00a.m.-4:00p.m. Monday-Sunday there may be someone around to answer some questions you may have regarding the farm and/or the horses.

Fairgrounds:
451 Eagle Avenue Hanover, PA 17331

"We have 4 main barns which you may go through, 2 of the barns are our stallion barns and the other two house the mares and their foals. The best time to see the mares and their foals up close is in the springtime."
Hanover Shoe Farms is located approximately 3 miles from the Hanover Square, halfway between Hanover and Littlestown on Route 194 South on the right hand side.
website, op cit.

* Mr Myers' Trees (courtesy of the Hanover Area Historical Society)

The Hanover Area Historical Society received the gift of the Warehime-Myers mansion in 2007. One stipulation in the gift was that the Society "preserve" the property. This has been a goal of HAHS...we work with an arborist... Considering the size of the three properties, we can surmise that Mr. Myers was extremely interested in trees – native and exotic trees. Also, we must keep in mind that this was the Edwardian Age in England and there were many British influences that made their way to America. The Edwardian Age began in 1901 with the death of Queen Victoria and the ascension of Edward VII to the throne and lasted for approximately 30 years. During those beginning years of the 20th Century the British Empire still maintained the enormous influence worldwide that it enjoyed under Queen Victoria. Britain was a hub for expanding global trade and a side benefit of this was the international movement of plants from far-away countries. Many plant explorers made difficult expeditions to china, Japan, and other mountainous and exotic areas to bring back to Britain, and then to America, the newest plant discoveries.

For the British that could afford it, gardening became the passion of those who had country estates and the means to employ gardeners to care for their land and plantings. Foreign influences inspired Japanese gardens, rock gardens, and alpine plantings...Homes had solariums, conservatories, and greenhouses to fill with exotic houseplants that we still use today – palms, ferns, African violets, and orchids.

Other factors in the spread of gardens and gardening were the photography industry, large scale printing industry, and an improved postal system. Inevitably all this interest in gardening spread to America where it was embraced by the people who were living on large tracts of land just beyond the crowded and industrial sections of towns and cities; many of these large houses/mansions were still within walking distance of the factories and the owners could walk home for lunch.

Old postcards and photographs show us what gardens looked like in the early 1900's. Unfortunately we have few pictures of the Myers mansion grounds at that time, but the size and approximate age of the trees at all three locations indicate that Mr. C.N. Myers began acquiring trees before 1920. His house was completed in 1913 and as time went on he acquired a larger lawn to the south of the house and planted trees as more room became available. He would also have planted boxwoods as landscape plants surrounding the mansion (these were still here in the '60s and '70's.) The gardens, as far as we know, were purely decorative – not vegetable gardens. The Myers family would have had a farm or farmers to supply food for the family and servants.

Some trees have been removed recently from the yard due to disease: A Magnolia that has been replaced, the two European Beeches are being replaced, and some hemlocks that succumbed to Wooly Adelgids...Prudent pruning is our preferred method of preserving the trees.

In the 1920's, Mr Myers...acquired the land across the alley from the Mansion and made a garden for his wife Ethel. The original use of this land was what we now call a landfill...more trees and shrubs were planted. By now, he was acquiring trees to the extent that he needed yet another piece of property. That piece is now the arboretum along Rte. 194 (near the Hanover Shoe Farms) That arboretum originally had over 700 trees and shrubs....there remain approximately 500 or fewer plants. It is still a remarkable collection...at one time it contained 6 trees that did not appear in any other arboretum; 9 trees that were in only one other arboretum; and 14 trees that were in only 3 other arboretum...the original list and plot placement of the trees in all three locations is still in existence.

The Myers Arboretum in Hanover Borough is now owned by the Borough and is a public park. Beech trees must have been a favorite because there were originally 10 European Beeches of various cultivars. The most impressive...are the Tri-color Beech and the Cut-Leaf Beech; they are planted close together and form a haven, along with a purple beech, that puts a person in an almost dark, cool space. There are also two American beeches that produce huge quantities of beechnuts. A rare beech called Beech Rotundifolia has round purple leaves instead of the pointed beech leaf. The common lifespan of a beech tree is about 100 years old so allof these trees are reaching the ends of their lives. There are also seven kinds of oak trees, each with its distinctive acorn....a Yellowood and a Katsura...

By the time Mr.Myers died in 1954, he had raised many trees from seed, planted 40 acres of spruce and pine at St. Bartholomew's church and 40 acres of walnut trees across the road from the same church. Mr. Myers and Mr.

Sheppard planted two million evergreens at the Sheppard and Myers water dam. Many of these trees have been harvested over the years.

The grounds of the Warehime-Myers Mansion and the Myers Arboretum Public Park are open to the public during daylight hours for strolling, picture-taking, or just enjoying the variety and majesty of mature trees that are truly beautiful.

*see Frank Goodyear's essay about the Millers, in Exhibitions section, for more on Peter's memoirs.

Chapter Three –

* Note that Teddy Roosevelt was a friend and colleague of Pennsylvania's Gifford Pinchot, both being governors of adjacent states in 1898-1900. TDR shared his conservationist views and love of nature with Pinchot. They drew attention to conservation of forests and streams at the First National governors' conference, themed "conservation." One can assume that the emphasis on trees as sustainable crops and for watersheds influenced the Sheppard-Myers plan to forest the hills around the Impounding Dam at Hanover.

* Edith's health was never robust. Early in her Western life, she stayed and worked at the Tilden School for Teaching Health in Denver, CO, a rather Spartan facility for stress-relief and healthy eating. She wrote articles for their *Philosophy of Health* magazine in the late 1920's.

*Tewa, see chapter one article on Tewa in notes.

*Edith's writings: Edith Warner is first listed as a writer in the WPA Guide to the SW, and she had many articles, essays and journals published, as many as eight in publications that no longer exist. Patrick Burns' *In the Shadow of Los Alamos* has gone into much greater detail.

* Co-incidence? Dasburg's niece, Peggy Harrison, moved to Hanover, PA in 1958. Her husband James, an internationally known harness racing writer and horse breeding executive, worked for the Hanover Shoe Farms and eventually the Lana Lobell Farms, They bought my Grandmother Miller's house on Baer Ave., and loaned many original Dasburgs for exhibit at the Hanover Public Library in the late 1970's. The author was the Arts Coordinator for the library.

Chapter Four –

*Another interesting coincidence: Edward Jones, a Manhattan Project mathematician, brought his family to Hanover, PA. and lived modestly just a few doors away from the Myers' mansion on Hanover St. He was our Junior High School principal, loved *The Charge of the Light Brigade* (which he showed repeatedly at assemblies), and was a brilliant and enthusiastic algebra teacher. His wife, Margaret, brought Shakespeare to life for us, as well. The author wonders if they somehow met Peter Miller through associates and chose her idyllic hometown to retreat to, post-war.

*The Barnes Foundation – Albert Barnes was born to wealth, in the late 19th Century, the end of the Industrial Revolution. Europe was full of change and growth, and the *belle époque* (beautiful age)was full tilt in Paris. Social unrest and class struggles were shown in the work of artists, and art was quite political. The beginnings of a rejection of realism came about through new techniques and abstraction – a new modern art. Barnes began collecting in 1912, with his close friend and artist William Glackens acting as his "buyer" for works by Van Gogh, Picasso, Renoir, and Cezanne. He became one of the biggest supporters of Modern Art, establishing his private museum at his home in Merion hall. It has recently moved to downtown Philadelphia, leaving behind in suburban Philadelphia only the arboretum, open to the public. The Barnes Collection is hung "salon style" in groupings unusual for its day, but fitting his philosophy of education in the arts, mixing old masters and modern art.
info@barnesfoundation.org
2025 Benjamin Franklin Parkway,Philadelphia, PA 19130; 215.278.7000

300 North Latch's Lane, Merion, PA 19066; 215.278.7350

*Charles Courtney Curran essay by James Lancel McElhinney: http://www/nccsc.net/essay/charles-courtney-curran#sthash.PBGJpV1W.dpuf

* _Abstract Painting Explained_ –by Andrea M. Theisson, copyright 2008.
Form and color alone are the two main hallmarks of Abstract Painting. Russian Wassily Kandinsky was perhaps the first to fully verbalize and show this, with his "Improvisations," painted around 1910 - 1915. Many others followed – Mondrian, Stella, Leger, Klee, Duchamp, de Kooning along with Pablo Picasso, who was the most prolific and outstanding of the early 20th Century movement. They all evolved from the earlier Fauves and Expressionists, yet took the analysis of shapes and synthesis of colors another step – to a more pure abstraction, or separation, from reality. It was an exciting time, and they fed off of each other's processes.

Many wrote letters, treatises and manifestos - such as this by Kandinsky, written in 1910: "A largely unconscious, spontaneous expression of inner character, of non-material nature. This I call an Improvisation.....Cold calculation, random spots of colour, mathematically exact construction (clearly shown or concealed), drawing that is now silent and now strident, painstaking thoroughness, colours like a flourish of trumpets or a pianissimo on the violin, great, calm, oscillating, splintered surfaces. Is this not form? Is this not 'the means?'...To speak of mystery in terms of mystery. Is this not content? Is this not the conscious and unconscious goal of the compelling urge to create.?...We feel sorry for those whose souls are deaf to the voice of art."**

Eventually, the color field paintings of Hans Hofmann and the action paintings of Pollock, Morris and Frankenthaler developed in the mid-century. Scale and materials shifted, yet the cerebral complexity behind the artists seemingly spontaneous work remained part of this very simplified visual experience. Abstract Painting achieved a universal acknowledgement in the Art world, as psychology also gained recognition over this dynamic century. I believe that only the first-person accounts by the artists are acceptable explanations of motive or intent. Yet, we can all appreciate this art in the context of society, and the evolution of culture.

Interestingly, most of these artists were actually trained professionally in representative, classic techniques. They became so moved by the spontaneous gesture of a thought process, a more considered aesthetic, a philosophy of perception, that they developed their individual styles. These are extremely diverse. This was done with awareness, growing more obvious as media and communications became more global. Europeans and Americans alike thrived upon the publicity of their new art form. Color Theory became part of the contemporary Art School curriculum, as did inclusion of the latest Abstractions in the major museums. They 'arrived.' The basic appreciation of composition and form, delight in the colors and the motion, contrasts and craftsmanship or surface have made this approach to painting a permanent and valid genre in the great world of Visual Art.

**from Letters of the Great Artists; Richard Friedenthal; vol. 2, pp 202-204; c. 1963 Random House

Chapter Five –

*Shirley Sherry article in The Evening Sun, Hanover PA; A Peek Inside One of Hanover's Twin Mansions, April 30, 1986. Courtesy archives of HAHS, Yellen Research Library.
*Obituary clipping, from Evening Sun and Peter's Memorial Service courtesy of Bill Richards

Copyright/Reprint permissions:
Brandywine River Museum of Art and Conservancy
Frank Goodyear Jr.
Hanover Area Historical Society
Jean and Lulien Levy Foundation for the Arts

Acknowledgments

I dedicate this book to all the wonderful, eccentric, artsy, rainbow-creative women whom I knew, still know, and will always love:
Mary Hoffman Miller (mother, artist, gardener, reader,) Trudi Hoffman Hollinger(aunt, painter, gardener, thinker,) Peg Hoffman Little (aunt, photographer-sculptor, gardener,) Henrietta "Peter" Myers Miller (friend of the family, absentee-mentor), Ruth "Jennifer" Kump Bargelt Chapin (in-law and friend, mentor), Justine Landis (teacher, artist, friend, historian,) Pat Masemer Good (neighbor, friend, networker), Ellie Winebrenner Naill (neighbor, agent-provocateur, entrepreneur), Denny Naill Piccola (partner-in-crime, patron of the arts, constant friend and optimist), Susan Hollinger Burch (cousin, artist), Joan Elizabeth Morton (friend, muse, and artist,) Patti Quinn Chapin (friend, patron of arts, stand-up comic, and urban connection,) Adele Fredette Theisson (ex-in-law and patron of art, mentor), Mary Ellen Hubbard (friend, artist, and mentor), Priscilla Greco McFerren (friend, actress, mentor, grandmother, and dynamo,) Jane Geiselman (friend, collector and fashionista,) Calder Ann Hollinger (dynamo, spirit-guide, and western aficionado, horsewoman, craftsperson,) Ann Roth (costume designer, native of Hanover, example), Joan Tucker Brittain-Wolff (professor, writer, astrologist, mentor,) Arlyn Pettingell (artist, painter, and pioneer,) Christine Muratore (artist, pioneer, and dynamo,) Karen Huston (Hanover artist & convert, friend), Rita Mae Brown (wildly creative author and inspiring native of Hanover, PA,) and many, many more! And the men who mentored, encouraged, or instigated: Alfred Young Wolff, Herb Leopold, Robert Rogers, John Moore, Rudolf Staffel, Bill Hollinger, Cliff Pfaff, Don Hubbard, Ron Cubbison, Lester Stone, Kim Potter, Bill Andrew,
Please see the extensive resources. bibliiography, and list of writers & their titles. I read, therefore I think. A recommended reading list is offered to include those stellar writers who have been guides, agents-provocateurs, lifesavers over the years. Also, I must include some websites and organizations that show tremendous hope for the Aquarian Conspiracy of the artist-eco-survivalists of the world. Special thanks to many, as well, who helped specifically with this effort : Liz Osbourne, Gail Stanislaw at the Brandywine Conservancy, Marilyn Batts (aka Leah Stravinsky, sculptor), Jim Schuman of the Hanover Area Historical Society, Marie DiFilippantonio of the Levy Gallery , James McEllhinney, Sharon Snyder of Los Alamos Historical Society, Bill Richards, Joe Rishel at the Philadelphia Museum of Art, Jeffrey and Beth Valocchi, Pat Burns, Frank Goodyear, Sharon Udall, Karen Findling - another extensive list! I must mention Madge Rohrbaugh Mitchell and her indomitable memory for names and faces of Hanover. And so many relatives and my artist-cousins, who have busy lives, but took time to dig out old memories and photos, and to share their treasures: Carol Hollinger, Christa Bargelt McInturff, Betsy Hollinger Rost. And the last-minute people who were working over the holidays of 2014 at Brandywine and P.A.F.A. And a couple of guys who ate a lot of frozen pizza over the holidays.

Bless you all!

About the Author:

" Art is meditation is play is process is Life…it's about remembering who you are, expressing the magic of simple pleasures, complex thoughts…
I am a paintweaver. (Thanks to Neil Welliver at the Vermont Studio Center) Life is Art and Art is Life. I celebrate this by painting and weaving the natural world with spirit, organic expressionism. I portray the simple enduring pleasures, little triumphs, comic relief. My own spirit-quest has touched upon places of intense power, fractal living, archetypal forces, new light and old souls. There are devas, druids and magic amongst us! I love color, texture, spontaneity…. I like to work in series, exploring directions, the light and shadows of life. "

This magna-cum-laude graduate of Tyler School of Art produces paintings and tapestries combining nature and the fractal thoughts of a lifetime… Organic expressionism, with spirit!

Her life is one of celebrating the arts, mindful living, wellness and supportive explorations….green networking, zen-lunacy and multi-mused amusement! She is also addicted to quotes, and loves books.

Her work includes multi-media art- paintings, watercolors, collage; tapestry; murals; herbals; papers and design; creative consultations, museum and display. She lives near Gettysburg, PA, and has a very messy studio.

Thank-you for sharing this story of many who should not be forgotten! So many old photos and papers, quality damaged, but saved!
Part of the proceeds will be donated to the Hanover Area Historical Society, and to conserve a farm-studio that Peter Miller would recognize.

Andrea

above: **Out of the Blues**, acrylic, 40"x20"

CPSIA information can be obtained at www.ICGtesting.com
Printed in the USA
LVIW01n1423110315
430141LV00011B/40